9/02

D0949525

MALARIA, WEST NILE, AND OTHER MOSQUITO-BORNE DISEASES

Other titles in Diseases and People

—Diseases and People—

MALARIA, WEST NILE, AND OTHER MOSQUITO-BORNE DISEASES

Nancy Day

Enslow Publishers, Inc.

40 Industrial Road PO Box 38
Box 398 Aldershot
Berkeley Heights, NJ 07922 Hants GU12 6BP
USA UK

http://www.enslow.com

Copyright © 2001 by Nancy Day

All rights reserved.

No part of this book may be reproduced by any means
without the written permission of the publisher.

Library of Congress Cataloging-in-Publication Data

Day, Nancy.
 Malaria, West Nile, and other mosquito-borne diseases / Nancy Day.
  p. cm. — (Diseases and people)
 Includes bibliographical references (p.) and index.
 ISBN 0-7660-1597-1
  1. Mosquitoes as carriers of disease—Juvenile literature.
 2. Malaria—Juvenile literature. 3. Yellow fever—Juvenile literature.
 [1. Mosquitoes as carriers of disease. 2. Malaria. 3. Yellow fever.
 4. Diseases.] I. Title. II. Series.
 RA640 .D39 2001
 614.4'323—dc21   00-009783

Printed in the United States of America

10 9 8 7 6 5 4 3 2 1

To Our Readers:
We have done our best to make sure all Internet addresses in this book were active and
appropriate when we went to press. However, the author and the publisher have no control
over and assume no liability for the material available on those Internet sites or on other
Web sites they may link to. Any comments or suggestions can be sent by e-mail to
comments@enslow.com or to the address on the back cover.

Illustration Credits: American Mosquito Control Association, pg. 25; Bristol-
Myers, Squibb, pp. 29, 39, 48, 50, 56, 75; Corel Corporation, pp. 10, 46, 64, 71,
77, 85, 93; Enslow Publishers, Inc., pg. 52; Gary Koellhoffer, pg. 69; National
Library of Medicine, pp. 13, 34, 36, 40, 42; Nancy Day, pp. 68, 87, 88; National
Institutes of Health, Dr. Robert Gwadz, pg. 23; Northern California
Comprehensive Sickle Cell Center, pg. 53; World Health Organization, pg. 62.

Cover Illustration: National Institutes of Health, Dr. Robert Gwadz.

614.4323
DAY
2001

Contents

Acknowledgments

I would like to thank the following individuals for their assistance:

Scott Campbell, Ph.D., entomologist, Suffolk County, New York Department of Health Services Arthropod-Borne Disease Laboratory.

Ray Dillon, DVM, MS, DACVIM, Jack O. Rash, professor of medicine, Department of Small Animal Surgery and Medicine, Auburn University, Alabama.

Robert Gwadz, Ph.D., assistant chief of the National Institute of Allergy and Infectious Diseases' Laboratory of Parasitic Diseases, Bethesda, Maryland.

Margaret Mackinnon, Ph.D., Institute of Cell, Animal, and Population Biology, University of Edinburgh, U.K.

Allan Platt, program coordinator, the Georgia Comprehensive Sickle Cell Center at Grady Health System, Atlanta, Georgia.

MOSQUITO-BORNE DISEASES

What are they? Mosquito-borne diseases are illnesses that are spread by mosquitoes. Mosquitoes pick up viruses or other organisms when they bite infected animals. The mosquitoes pass on the organisms later when they bite other animals (including humans). Diseases such as West Nile virus, malaria, yellow fever, Rift Valley fever, dengue fever, and dog heartworm are a few of the diseases spread by mosquitoes. Mosquitoes can also spread some types of encephalitis, an inflammation of the brain or the tissues surrounding the brain. The infection can damage the brain. In severe cases, the patient dies. Most mosquito-borne diseases are zoonoses, or diseases that can be passed from animals to humans. Malaria is an unusual mosquito-borne disease in that it is passed only from humans to humans. There are animal forms of malaria, but these do not affect humans.

Who gets them? Mosquito-borne diseases affect humans of all ages and races, and both sexes. Some, such as malaria, can be serious or even fatal. People living in tropical areas, particularly in Africa, Asia, and South America, are most at risk. However, outbreaks of mosquito-borne diseases can occur almost anywhere, as we witnessed recently when incidents of West Nile virus appeared in and around the New York City metropolitan area. Mosquito-borne diseases also harm livestock such as cows and sheep, birds, monkeys, dogs, cats, rodents, and even snakes.

How do you get infected? Female mosquitoes bite animals (including humans) to get a meal of blood. The mosquitoes need the protein found in animal blood to feed themselves and to nourish their eggs. When female mosquitoes bite animals infected with certain diseases, the blood they take in will contain disease-causing organisms.

In many cases, the animal serves as a reservoir—a place that provides a continuing supply of organisms. An animal that acts as a reservoir is often unharmed by the disease. When the organisms are picked up from a reservoir by a mosquito, they begin to multiply inside the mosquito. Eventually, they make their way to the mosquito's salivary glands. Then, when the mosquito bites its next victim, it first injects saliva to numb the area. During this process, it can pass any disease-causing organisms in its saliva to the new victim, who is called a host.

In the case of malaria, humans serve as both the reservoir and the host, so the disease is only carried from human to human. Other diseases can by carried from monkeys or other animals to humans. These are called zoonoses.

What are the symptoms? Symptoms vary according to the disease. Some conditions are so mild that people may never even know they are infected. Others are serious, causing high fever, cycles of chills and fever, hemorrhaging (bleeding), encephalitis, and even death.

How are they treated? Treatment also varies by disease. For many years, people have used quinine, a substance that comes from the bark of the cinchona tree, to treat malaria. In recent years, new drugs have been developed, but there is still no certain cure. For some mosquito-borne diseases, such as Rift Valley fever, drugs commonly used to treat illnesses caused by viruses may help. For other diseases, all that can be done is to treat the symptoms and replace body fluids lost through hemorrhaging or sweating.

How can they be prevented? Mosquito-borne diseases can be prevented by using netting or other screening material to keep mosquitoes from making direct contact with people, or by discouraging the presence of mosquitoes with repellents. Repellents containing diethyl toluamide (DEET) prevent mosquitoes from sensing the human body. Wearing lightweight, white clothing also helps discourage mosquitoes (they are attracted by color and by body heat). People can avoid some mosquito bites by remaining indoors, especially when the sun begins to set, the time when many mosquitoes are active. In addition, mosquito populations can be reduced by killing mosquitoes with insecticides or by draining the watery areas where they breed. Vaccines are available to protect people and animals against some mosquito-borne diseases. For other diseases, scientists are working to find safe and effective vaccines.

New York City and surrounding areas became the focus of attention in the summer of 1999 due to an outbreak of West Nile virus.

1

West Nile in New York City

In the summer of 1999, Deborah Asnis, chief of infectious diseases at Flushing Hospital in New York City, was concerned about three patients who shared an unusual combination of symptoms. They were burning with fever, confused, and so weak they could not move. Some of the symptoms pointed to pneumonia, a lung infection. But why were their muscles so weak? She started to think they might have some kind of encephalitis, an inflammation of the brain, but their symptoms did not match those normally seen with encephalitis, either.

At the same time, only a short distance away, Tracey McNamara, head of the department of pathology (which studies diseases) at the Wildlife Conservation Society at the Bronx Zoo, began hearing that crows were dying at an alarming rate in the neighborhoods around the zoo. When dead crows started showing up on the zoo grounds, she became concerned. Zoo animals can pick up diseases from local wildlife. McNamara sent some of the dead birds to the state Department of Environmental Conservation for medical analysis.[1]

Back in Flushing, two Health Department physicians, Marcelle Layton and Annie Fine, visited Asnis's patients. It was the end of August, and the number of patients with unexplained symptoms had grown to five. Layton sent specimens from the patients to the Centers for Disease Control and Prevention (CDC) in Atlanta for testing. These specimens tested positive for St. Louis encephalitis, a disease mosquitoes can transmit from birds to humans.[2]

People were stunned. A rare mosquito-borne virus in New York City? It seemed like a science fiction movie come to life. But as some patients died and more cases popped up, officials scrambled. They needed to try to do something to control the spread of the virus and calm the worried local population. Mayor Rudolph Giuliani announced that the city would begin a massive spraying program to kill mosquitoes. Trucks and helicopters blanketed New York City and surrounding areas with a fog of pesticides. While some residents protested the use of powerful chemicals over such a wide area, others feared that the epidemic would spread rapidly, causing many deaths. Some people did not know which to fear more—the disease or the preventive measures.

Meanwhile, at the Bronx Zoo, McNamara was still concerned. Since St. Louis encephalitis does not affect the birds

At the sprawling Centers for Disease Control and Prevention complex in Atlanta, Georgia, teams of experts work to prevent and contain outbreaks of infectious diseases.

that carry it, that diagnosis did not explain what was killing the crows. Then, on Labor Day weekend, the zoo's own rare birds began to die. McNamara knew she had to find the problem quickly. She sent specimens to the United States Department of Agriculture's National Veterinary Services Laboratories in Ames, Iowa, but they tested negative for all of the most likely diseases. Then on September 16, while using an electron microscope to examine a specimen, the Iowa researchers found tiny pieces of virus that seemed to point to the *Flavivirus* family, the group of viruses that includes St. Louis encephalitis.[3]

Toward the end of September, health officials in New York City were still finding new human cases, and three people had died. They sent samples of the dead patients' brains to the Emerging Diseases Laboratory at the University of California, Irvine, for closer examination. On the morning of September 23, the California researchers told the startled New York health officials that their mystery disease was not St. Louis encephalitis, just as they had suspected. It did, however, look a lot like a disease caused by a closely related organism—the Kunjin/West Nile virus. CDC researchers reexamined their samples and reached the same conclusion. The New York patients were suffering from West Nile virus, a disease rarely seen outside Africa, Australia, and the Middle East. When the researchers analyzing McNamara's bird specimens tested them in the laboratory for the West Nile virus, they found a match. The mystery was solved.[4]

West Nile virus had popped up from time to time in Europe (there were outbreaks in the western Mediterranean area and southern Russia in 1962–1964, Belarus and Ukraine in the 1970s, Romania in 1996–1997, and Italy in 1998). But it had never before been seen in the Western Hemisphere.[5]

Suffolk County, Long Island, not far from New York City, was one of the areas where officials applied pesticides in an effort to prevent the spread of West Nile virus. The county had a decades-old surveillance (monitoring) program that routinely trapped and examined mosquitoes. Their program was designed to detect eastern equine virus, the most serious virus in the area up until the summer of 1999. Naturally, the Suffolk County program did not identify the West Nile virus because it was not testing for it. After all, West Nile virus had never been seen before in North America.

Entomologist (a scientist who studies insects) Scott Campbell, of the Suffolk County Department of Health Services Arthropod-Borne Disease Laboratory, explains: "The number of arboviruses [a family of viruses that are often carried by insects] out there are too numerous just to say O.K., we'll check them, we'll check them all. You can't afford to do something like that. So you check basically what you intend to find." When the first reports came out in late September that West Nile virus had been identified, Campbell said, "Obviously there was some horror as well as scientific interest. How did it get here? What's the best way to do surveillance? What species was the virus in? So there were many, many different aspects that had to be looked at. Obviously people had died, so there was much concern about individuals possibly being exposed to the virus. So there was a lot of activity with regard to surveillance and control."[6]

Although West Nile virus is not one of the more lethal mosquito-borne diseases, experts estimated that the 1999 New York outbreak made sixty-two people sick and killed seven.[7] There was also concern because *Culex pipiens*, the mosquito that was the primary carrier of West Nile, is the most common species of mosquito in urban areas, including those found in North America.

So how did the West Nile virus get to New York? Officials think that a mosquito, bird, or human host carried it there. In November 1999, experts at a workshop in Fort Collins,

15

Colorado, announced that DNA tests performed on samples of the virus showed that the New York epidemic was definitely caused by the West Nile virus. They also determined that the genetic makeup of the virus that caused the New York outbreak was nearly identical to a West Nile strain found in Israel a year earlier.

"There's a lot of traffic between the Middle East and the New York area," explains John Roehrig, the scientist at the CDC laboratory for arboviral diseases in Fort Collins, Colorado, who led the study that positively identified the West Nile virus. "We may never know exactly what happened."[8]

Public health officials are more worried about the future than the past: Will West Nile virus become an ongoing problem for the northeastern United States? In February 2000, the New Jersey Department of Health was concerned enough to apply for a federal grant of nearly $250,000 to track mosquitoes and birds that might carry the West Nile virus. The CDC had offered $2.5 million to sixteen states to aid in tracking efforts, and New Jersey wanted to be sure it got part of that sum. Experts were concerned that migrating birds had carried West Nile virus south as they traveled. In October 1999, officials identified a dead crow with the disease in Baltimore, Maryland. Even though there were no cases of West Nile in humans that far south, the discovery caused concern that there might be in the future.

The New York outbreak occurred at the end of the summer and ended as cold weather sent mosquitoes into hiding

16

for the winter. Nevertheless, scientists worried that mosquitoes carrying the disease might spend the winter in New York's subway system and other protected areas. "The worst case scenario is that it's going to spread all over the eastern U.S. and we [will] face outbreaks every year," said David Morens, of the National Institute of Allergy and Infectious Diseases in Bethesda, Maryland.[9]

In March 2000, federal health inspectors got the first clue that their fears might come true. They tested hibernating mosquitoes collected from areas around New York City. Three specimens contained traces of the West Nile virus. "This does not necessarily mean the disease is coming back when it warms up in the New York area," said Dr. Stephen M. Ostroff, associate director at the National Center for Infectious Diseases in Atlanta. "But this raises the possibility that it might."[10] In the meantime, New York City planned to launch mosquito control efforts by April. "We have got to kill as many of those critters as possible," said Mayor Giuliani.[11]

By the summer of 2000, West Nile was back in the New York area. In July, mosquitoes in the heart of Manhattan tested positive for the virus, causing the cancellation of a New York Philharmonic concert in Central Park. Scientists concluded that West Nile virus is here to stay. "We're beyond containment now," said Robert G. McLean, a government biologist studying West Nile's effect on birds. "We have to live with it and do the best we can."[12]

2
Mosquitoes and Disease

Even though they are only a few millimeters long, mosquitoes could be considered the most dangerous animals in the world. The World Health Organization (WHO) estimates that mosquitoes infect up to 700 million people a year and are responsible for the deaths of more than 2 million of those infected.[1]

Up until recently at least, most people in the United States thought of mosquitoes as nothing more than pests that can spoil a summer picnic. But in other parts of the world, mosquitoes are known to create widespread epidemics that wipe out livestock, devastate families, and affect the economic growth of entire countries. The recent epidemics of mosquito-borne diseases in New York and other areas have made Americans more aware of the dangers mosquitoes can carry. Although small in size, mosquitoes have caused problems throughout human history (they played a role in the decline of ancient Greece, the sale of the Louisiana Territory, and the loss of millions of soldiers during times of war) and continue to be a major problem even now.

No one has actually counted, but it has been estimated that at any given moment about 100 trillion mosquitoes are buzzing around the world.[2] Some of them can fly as far as one hundred miles away, while others stick close to home. To be

Which Disaster Is the Biggest Killer?

Earthquakes, floods, hurricanes, tornadoes, wars: they are all killers. But what kind of disaster kills the most people? A far less dramatic one: infectious disease. Just three diseases (AIDS, tuberculosis, and malaria) have killed an estimated 150 million people since 1945. During that same period, 23 million died in wars. Television, magazines, and newspapers are filled with dramatic coverage of natural disasters, yet preventable disease kills far more people. In 1999 alone, the death toll from infectious diseases was 160 times greater than from that year's violent earthquakes in Turkey, cyclones in India, and floods in Venezuela. These statistics have forced the Red Cross to take another look at their disaster relief work. They are finding that providing clothes, shelter, and food to disaster victims is only part of the story. Providing preventive health care and aid for health education are also critical in order to save lives.[3]

19

SIMMS LIBRARY ALBUQUERQUE ACADEMY

able to survive, mosquitoes need warmth, water, and blood. Most carry no diseases at all, and some mosquito-borne diseases are so mild that people can have them without knowing it. But others are deadly.

There are a variety of diseases spread by mosquitoes, but the one with the greatest impact is malaria. In many wars, including the Civil War (1861–1865) and the Vietnam War (1964–1975), malaria caused more casualties than bullets.[4] In fact, taking into account all of recorded history, malaria has affected more people than any other infectious disease. Moreover, this disease is far from extinct. As recently as 1999, over one million people died from malaria. That figure translates into three thousand people a day.[5]

Anatomy of a Mosquito

There is one easy way to tell if a mosquito is male or female: if it bites you, it is female. A male mosquito has never bitten anyone—the males just do not have the right equipment.

Mosquitoes are insects. They are classified within the order known as *Diptera,* the "true flies." Of the more than one hundred thousand species of *Diptera* in the world, about three thousand of them belong to the family called *Culicidae,* the mosquitoes. One detail that makes mosquitoes different from other flies is that their wings have scales. The other is that female mosquitoes have long, piercing mouthparts that can penetrate skin.

Female mosquitoes puncture the skin of certain animals (including humans) and draw out blood (on average, about one-thousandth of a teaspoon, or 0.005 milliliter.)[6] The blood provides the protein that mosquitoes need to nurture, or feed, their eggs. The red blood cells, or the solid part of the blood, provides this protein. The more of this blood protein the females get, the more eggs they can lay. In some species of mosquitoes, the females cannot even form eggs until they get a blood meal first. A few species of mosquitoes do not feed on blood at all, and because of this adaptation, they cannot transmit disease.

Male mosquitoes do not need a biting mouth. They eat flower nectar and liquids that come from rotting vegetation. Most of the time, that is what the females eat, too. But when it comes time to make eggs, these females go looking for blood.

Types of Mosquitoes

If you live in the United States, you have seen only a fraction of the different species of mosquitoes. Of the three thousand species throughout the world, only about one hundred seventy different kinds are found in the United States.[7] Some species are better known than others, particularly for their ability to transmit disease.

You will know if an *Aedes* mosquito bites you—it will hurt! This species bites mainly during the dawn and dusk periods, and prefers mammals like humans to other animals. *Aedes sollicitans*, the salt marsh mosquito, can fly more than ten miles. It can carry eastern equine encephalitis, a disease that affects animals but can also be deadly in humans. *Aedes triseriatus*, known as the tree-hole mosquito, carries LaCrosse encephalitis. In the 1970s and early 1980s, the LaCrosse type of encephalitis was the leading disease spread by arthropods (the family of organisms that includes mosquitoes and ticks).[8] Then Lyme disease (an illness spread by ticks) took the lead.

Aedes albopictus, the Asian tiger mosquito, was first seen in the United States in Memphis, Tennessee, in 1983. It traveled to America by hitching a ride inside used tires that were imported from Asia. Since that time, it has spread to twenty-five states, from Illinois to Florida (it has also established colonies in Cuba, South America, and even Italy).[9] It can carry encephalitis and dengue fever.

Aedes aegypti arrived in America much earlier. This mosquito traveled aboard ships transporting slaves from Africa in the 1600s and 1700s. Once it arrived in America, *Aedes aegypti* began to spread yellow fever, causing devastating epidemics. *Aedes aegypti* also carries dengue and dengue hemorrhagic fever. It is now an indoor mosquito that rarely goes outside.

The bite of the *Culex* mosquito is also quite painful. These mosquitoes bite around sunset and after dark, but they prefer birds to mammals. They will enter buildings looking for a blood meal, but do not fly far from home. *Culex nigripalpus* can transmit encephalitis to humans and horses and is found in Florida as well as other parts of the world. *Culex pipiens* was the mosquito responsible for the 1999 outbreak of West Nile virus in the New York metropolitan area. American scientists are keeping their eyes on other types of *Culex* as well. In Israel, India, and other places, West Nile virus is carried by other species of *Culex,* so there is every reason to suspect that other varieties of *Culex* in North America may begin transmitting the disease, too.

Although the different species of mosquitoes have individual characteristics, they can adapt to new conditions over time. For example, *Aedes aegypti* became city-dwelling, indoor creatures because they found it easier to find hosts in buildings. The mosquitoes moved inside houses, where they became dependent upon human blood and open containers of water for breeding. Then, after American homes got colder due to air conditioning and people installed plumbing rather than store water in open containers where mosquitoes can breed,

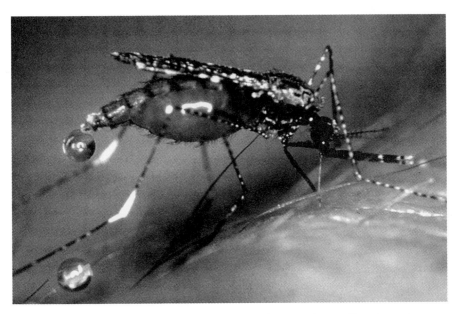

The *Aedes aegypti* mosquito, responsible for spreading yellow fever, is highly adaptable. The species moved outdoors after American homes began to store less water (due to better plumbing) and became cooler (due to air conditioning).

23

Aedes aegypti moved outdoors, and began to breed in yards. Some species have even adapted to cold climates, including the Arctic. They hibernate in the winter and breed in warm pools of melted snow.

The *Anopheles* mosquito carries malaria. *Anopheles gambiae* is the main carrier in tropical Africa, while *Anopheles albimanus* is the primary carrier in South and Central America. Other types of *Anopheles* mosquitoes have been responsible for malaria outbreaks in Turkey and Europe.

The Life of a Mosquito

Like many other insects, the mosquito's life goes through four stages. The word for this process of changes is *metamorphosis* and it means change. The four stages of this metamorphosis are: 1) egg, 2) larva, 3) pupa, and 4) adult.

A mosquito starts life just like the rest of us: as an egg. Some mosquitoes lay their eggs in water, where they float on the surface. One mosquito can produce between six to three hundred eggs at a time, depending upon the species and the amount of blood it took in.[10] Some mosquitoes lay eggs that stick together, forming a raft of a hundred or more eggs that floats on the surface of water. Other mosquitoes lay their eggs in areas that are dry but that will later be flooded by water. For example, the eggs of the salt marsh mosquito can survive for weeks, months, and even years, waiting for the water that allows them to hatch.

However, most mosquito eggs hatch and become larvae within forty-eight hours of being in water. Larvae live in the

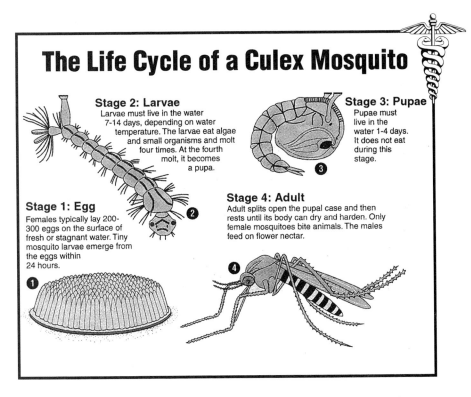

The Life Cycle of a Culex Mosquito

Stage 2: Larvae
Larvae must live in the water 7-14 days, depending on water temperature. The larvae eat algae and small organisms and molt four times. At the fourth molt, it becomes a pupa.

Stage 3: Pupae
Pupae must live in the water 1-4 days. It does not eat during this stage.

Stage 1: Egg
Females typically lay 200-300 eggs on the surface of fresh or stagnant water. Tiny mosquito larvae emerge from the eggs within 24 hours.

Stage 4: Adult
Adult splits open the pupal case and then rests until its body can dry and harden. Only female mosquitoes bite animals. The males feed on flower nectar.

water but breathe air. Some do this with the help of a straw-like breathing tube that breaks the water's surface while they hang below it. Others lie on the surface of the water and breathe through an opening in their bodies. Larvae feed on microorganisms and algae, or tiny plants, in the water. The larvae molt, or shed their skins, four times. They grow larger each time, until they reach the pupa stage at the fourth molt.

At the pupa stage, which is similar to the cocoon for a butterfly, the mosquito develops gradually into an adult. It does not eat, but it breathes through two tubes called trumpets. After about two days, the pupa breaks open, and the adult mosquito emerges. It rests on the water while its body dries and hardens. It cannot fly until its wings are dry.

Like many insects, the female mosquito needs to mate only once. She stores the male's sperm in her body. After that she can fertilize her own eggs every time she lays them, which may be as often as every three days. As long as she gets a blood meal to nourish each batch of newly produced eggs, she can continue to create offspring.

The mosquito life cycle is affected by temperature. For example, *Culex tarsalis*, a mosquito common in California, completes the cycle in fourteen days when it is 70 degrees outside, but in only ten days at 80 degrees.[11] The length of the mosquito life cycle also varies by species. Some complete the cycle in only four days, while others take an entire month.

The length of an adult female mosquito's life is important because if the mosquito bites an infected animal and then lives long enough to bite another animal it will pass along the disease-carrying organism. That female then becomes a vector, or a means of spreading disease. The length of the female mosquito's life also directly affects the size of the mosquito population. The longer a female lives, the more offspring she can produce. With the right amount of warmth and water, mosquitoes can reproduce at an astonishing rate. A single female mosquito can produce up to one thousand offspring in its short lifetime.[12]

Most mosquitoes survive during the winter in the egg stage, waiting for the water to warm. Then the eggs hatch, and the life cycle begins. Some female mosquitoes that have already stored sperm in their bodies can live through the winter, resting in basements, sewers, well pits, or other cool, protected locations. When the weather warms, they look for a blood meal and begin to lay eggs. A very few species can wait out the winter as larvae.

Hosts and Vectors: The Cycle of Disease Transmission

A vector is an organism that picks up a disease from a reservoir (an animal that carries a continuing supply of disease-causing organisms), carries the disease-causing organisms within or on the surface of its body, and then infects another animal. Insects that bite are common vectors because they make efficient transmitters of disease. Other insect vectors are fleas, lice, ticks, and flies.

A mosquito takes on disease-causing organisms, such as viruses or parasites, when it sucks the blood from an animal source. The organisms multiply inside the mosquito's body, using the mosquito to complete a part of their own life cycle. From there, they infect cells in various tissues and organs of the mosquito, eventually traveling to its salivary glands, the organs that produce saliva.

When the female mosquito bites, two sharp cutting tools called stylets, located on the mosquito's mouth, pierce the victim's skin. Then two tiny tubes search beneath the victim's skin for small blood vessels called capillaries. When the mosquito locates a capillary, it sends saliva down one tube, called the hypopharynx (the saliva contains substances to numb the area, widen the capillary, and keep the blood flowing). Then it sucks the animal's blood up through the other tube, called the labrum. Infected blood from one animal is never passed directly to another victim while the mosquito is feeding because when the mosquito bites, the blood flows in only one direction (into the mosquito). The only thing that is passed to the person being bitten is the mosquito's saliva (which travels down a tube separate from the tube used to take in blood). This is one reason why HIV (the virus that causes AIDS) and many other disease-causing organisms that can be present in blood are not passed to other hosts through mosquito bites. The mosquito's mouthparts are much more complicated than a hypodermic needle.

Viruses or other disease-causing organisms are injected into a host with the mosquito's saliva. This can only happen if the organism is already present in the mosquito's salivary glands. An allergic reaction to the saliva produces the itchy bump that is left behind.

Fortunately, few mosquito bites transmit disease-causing organisms. Infectious organisms must be present in the salivary glands of the mosquito before they can be passed on to another host. Not many mosquitoes live longer than a week, so many die before they can transmit the disease. Only the female mosquito bites, and even then, she only bites when she needs blood to develop eggs. In addition, mosquitoes like the Asian Tiger mosquito bite many different kinds of animals. If the mosquitoes are busy biting nonhuman animals, any disease they might be carrying will not be passed to humans.

How a Mosquito Bites

1. The Sting
Sharp mouth parts called stylets pierce the victim's skin. Sometimes a mosquito probes several times before finding blood. Each thrust may take ten seconds.

2. The Itch
As stylets enter skin, the labium bends and slides up and out of the way. Saliva flows down the hypopharynx tube and into the wounds made by the stylets. Saliva keeps the blood from clotting. Many humans are allergic to the saliva, which causes the wound to swell into an itchy welt.

3. The Blood
Blood is sucked up through the tubular labrum.

4. The Withdrawal
The mosquito slowly pulls its stylets out of the wound. The labium slips back into place over them.

5. The Getaway
The mosquito flies away.

Why Mosquitoes Cannot Transmit AIDS

To spread disease, a mosquito must first take in disease-causing organisms with its blood meal. The organisms must be able to survive inside the mosquito (and preferably increase in number). Then the organisms must get to the mosquito's salivary glands, from which location they are passed to a new host in the saliva that is injected while the mosquito takes its next blood meal. The mosquito never injects blood; it only injects saliva. It does this through a tube separate and distinct from the one that is taking in blood.

People infected with HIV, the virus that causes AIDS, have extremely low quantities of the HIV virus in their blood. In fact, 70 to 80 percent of infected people have no detectable levels of virus particles in their blood. In addition, the HIV virus, unlike mosquito-borne disease organisms, has no way to survive the mosquito's digestive system. Any HIV virus particles the mosquito does take in are digested like food in the mosquito's stomach, so they never get to the salivary glands. This means that to pass on HIV, the mosquito would have to bite an infected person, then bite another person immediately, and have enough virus left on its mouthparts to infect the other person. However, since virus levels in the blood are so low, the amount of blood that might be present on a mosquito's mouthparts is very small. For these reasons, scientists have estimated that it would take the bites of 10 million mosquitoes to transfer a single unit of HIV![13]

However, some mosquitoes have characteristics that make them more troublesome. *Aedes aegypti* mosquitoes, for example, live primarily indoors and have relatively long life spans. They are less annoying than other mosquitoes and are very sensitive to movement. They can start to draw blood without someone being aware of it, and then dart away before the person has a chance to swat them. They may bite several people in a row before they have their fill, infecting each one with whatever disease they are carrying. And they feed almost exclusively on humans, so few bites are "wasted" on other animals.

How can such a small pest continue to cause so many problems in the modern world? Changes in climate, growth of human populations, and a wider network of global transportation allow mosquitoes to move into new areas, carrying diseases with them. Mosquitoes can also become carriers for new types of diseases.

3

Mosquito-Borne Diseases in History

Malaria has been known since the beginning of recorded history. Yet it took thousands of years for anyone to recognize that the mosquito played a part in its spread.

The word malaria comes from the Greek words *mal*, meaning "bad," and *aria*, meaning "air." Malaria was common in ancient Greece, where it caused poor health, a falling birth rate, and low morale among the soldiers. In fact, historians think the famous conqueror Alexander the Great may have suffered with it, perhaps even dying from it while in Mesopotamia in the fourth century B.C.[1]

People realized that pools of dirty water seemed to be involved in the spread of the disease. But they thought that the smelly gasses produced by stagnant water were to blame. They did not understand that the dirty water made a perfect

32

breeding ground for mosquitoes. The threat of malaria was one reason the ancient Romans created drainage systems to get rid of standing water.[2]

Malaria was probably brought to the Americas by the European explorers and traders. In the early 1600s, native people in South America discovered that the bark of the cinchona tree cured malaria. They soaked this bark in water and then drank the foul-tasting broth.[3]

During the Civil War, mosquitoes (called "gallinippers" by the soldiers) were a major problem, particularly in the South, where most of the battles were fought. Malaria, which soldiers called "the shakes" due to the body-rattling chills it caused, became so common that in some army camps the usual greeting was "Have you had the shakes?" Still no one yet made the connection between mosquitoes and malaria. In the Union Army alone, there were over 1.3 million cases of malaria and ten thousand deaths. The North used over nineteen tons of quinine sulfate to treat malaria victims during the war. In the South, quinine became more valuable than gold (costing $400 to $600 an ounce) when Union blockades kept quinine supplies from getting through.[4]

The first person to prove the mosquito connection was Scottish doctor Patrick Manson, who was working in China between 1871 and 1890. He found that mosquitoes were able to pick up tiny young roundworms in the blood of patients suffering from elephantiasis, a disease that causes massive swelling of the arms, legs, and scrotum (the pouch that holds the testes). However, Manson believed each mosquito only

A Civil War field hospital near Petersburg, Virginia. During the war, more soldiers were felled by malaria than by gunfire.

took one blood meal in its lifetime, so he assumed it spread the disease by releasing the worms into drinking water or spreading them in populated areas. Each time scientists suggested that mosquitoes were responsible for spreading disease, people did not want to believe it. They found it hard to accept that such a small, unimportant creature could cause such serious problems.

In 1880, Alphonse Laveran, a French army surgeon who was stationed in Algiers, used a microscope to examine the blood of a soldier with malaria. He discovered that the soldier had a tiny type of parasite—a creature that lives in or on another organism and depends on it to live—in his blood.

Parasites

Parasites are plants or animals that depend on other living creatures. Some parasites use the other organism, called the host, for only a short period of time. Others cannot ever live apart from the host. Parasites are usually smaller than the host and of a different species. Most parasites do harm to their hosts.

Parasites affect nearly all life forms. Bacteria are used as hosts by some viruses. The common Christmas plant, mistletoe, is actually a parasite that takes its water and nutrients from other plants. More than one hundred parasites known to cause disease use humans as their hosts. Parasites come in a variety of forms. Viruses are entirely parasitic, able to survive and reproduce only within other living organisms.

In malaria, the mosquito transmits the infective larval stage of the malaria parasite to humans with its bite. The larvae reproduce in the human liver, producing a cyst, or small fluid-filled sac, that releases new larvae into the bloodstream. These larvae invade the host's red blood cells and reproduce, eventually breaking the blood cells open. When the blood cells break open, a toxin, or poison, is released. This is what causes the chills and fever that are the characteristic symptoms of malaria patients.

Dr. Ronald Ross, a British physician born in India, was the first to see the malaria parasite inside a mosquito under a microscope. He is responsible for the theory that mosquitoes spread malaria by injecting malaria parasites when they bite.

Even after this discovery, no one could figure out how the malaria parasites had gotten inside the soldier. At first, scientists thought the parasites might have come from the nearby foul-smelling marshes that people had blamed for malaria since ancient times, but they could not find the same parasites in the water.

In the 1890s, Ronald Ross, an India-born British doctor who had met Patrick Manson and become interested in malaria, went to India to study infected soldiers. While most experts rejected the idea that mosquitoes might spread the malaria parasite, Ross spent hour after hour, week after week, dissecting mosquitoes and studying them under a microscope. He also spent time learning about the parasite's life cycle and studying malaria in birds. Then in 1897, while looking at a dissected *Anopheles* mosquito under a microscope, he finally saw the malaria parasite (the organism that Alphose Laveran had seen in the blood of a soldier with malaria). Later, he

The Countess's Cure

Quinine, a drug that has been treating malaria for hundreds of years, comes from a type of evergreen tree, the cinchona (sometimes called chinchona), that is native to the Andes mountain region from Bolivia to Columbia, in South America, and the highlands of Panama and Costa Rica, in Central America. The bark of the cinchona, which the native people of Peru call *quina quina*, contains the bitter chemical we now know as quinine. The tree was named in honor of the Spanish countess of Chinchón who, according to legend, was cured of a fever in 1638 after being treated with the bark in South America. Afterward, she ordered the bark to be collected and sent back to Spain to help malaria patients there.

In 1820, French chemists isolated quinine as the active ingredient in cinchona bark. American chemists were able to create quinine in the laboratory through chemical synthesis in 1944, making it easier to produce large quantities of the drug. In addition to treating malaria, quinine has been used to reduce fever and pain, to trigger labor in pregnant women, as a hardening agent in the treatment of varicose (bulging) veins, and in soft drinks called tonics that are often mixed with alcoholic beverages.

figured out that mosquitoes spread malaria by injecting saliva containing malaria parasites into animals when they bite. For his work, Ross was awarded the 1902 Nobel Prize in medicine.[5]

From Cuba to the Canal

When American troops took control of Havana, Cuba, in 1899 after the Spanish American War, one of the first orders of business was to try to control the outbreak of yellow fever. Not only was the disease devastating Cuba, but ships taking sugar to North America might take yellow fever with them to American ports.

William Crawford Gorgas, an army major and medical doctor, was sent to clean up Havana. Thinking that yellow fever, like many other diseases, was bred in sewage and garbage, Gorgas first attacked the filth in the streets. When the epidemic continued, a new team, led by another medical major, Walter Reed, was sent to investigate.

Some twenty years earlier, Carlos Finlay, a Cuban doctor, had claimed that yellow fever was transmitted by "stegs," or *Stegomyia fasciata* mosquitoes, which are now known as *Aedes aegypti*. But Finlay had had no luck in proving this theory because he did not realize that the process of transmitting the disease required careful timing.

Walter Reed wanted to test the transmission of yellow fever by mosquitoes. Unfortunately, no animals were known to get yellow fever, so the only way the doctors could conduct experiments was with humans. Before the project was started,

Walter Reed was called back to the United States, but his associates, James Carroll, Jesse W. Lazear, and Aristides Agramonte pressed on.

They decided to start using themselves as guinea pigs. Dr. Lazear allowed mosquitoes to bite yellow fever patients and then bite his arm, but nothing happened. (The disease had not had enough time to develop inside the mosquito.) Four days later, Dr. Carroll did the same, and he got a severe case of yellow fever. However, the team needed more proof. Dr. Carroll might have picked up the disease from sick soldiers or their infected bedding, they reasoned. Then a soldier who had not had any contact with yellow fever victims volunteered for the experiment. When this soldier got sick after being bitten by mosquitoes, he became the first real proof that mosquitoes

This 1928 poster for the medicines of E.R. Squibb & Sons shows Dr. Walter Reed (center) in Cuba, searching for a cure for yellow fever.

spread yellow fever. Then Dr. Lazear was accidentally bitten and became ill. Unlike Dr. Carroll, Lazear did not survive.[6]

Still, more evidence was needed to prove that mosquito bites were the only way to spread yellow fever. The researchers set up two groups of soldier volunteers. One group lived among the soiled clothing and bedding of yellow fever victims, but they were protected from mosquitoes by netting. The other group was kept away from yellow fever victims, but they were exposed to mosquitoes that had bitten yellow fever patients. None of the first group got yellow fever, but 80 percent of those bitten by the infected mosquitoes got sick.[7]

The researchers found that when it came to contracting yellow fever, timing was everything. Mosquitoes can pick up the disease from patients only during their first three days of

infection. Then, it takes twelve to twenty days for the disease to develop inside the mosquito before it can be passed on to another victim.

After the biting experiments, Dr. Reed, who had returned to Cuba, and Dr. Gorgas decided to experiment with vaccines, or

Dr. Jesse W. Lazear died in Cuba, after volunteering to be bitten by mosquitoes that had already bitten yellow fever patients.

preparations made from living disease-carrying organisms. The doctors would vaccinate volunteers to see whether they could produce in the volunteers a mild case of yellow fever that would not make them too sick but would produce an immunity to the disease. After three of the seven volunteers died from this experiment, the doctors switched their efforts. Instead, they isolated infected patients so mosquitoes could not bite them (and pick up the disease), sprayed houses with insecticides, and drained mosquito breeding grounds. After these efforts, the number of cases of yellow fever in Havana dropped from 1,400 in 1900 to 37 in 1901.[8] As a bonus, the campaign also defeated malaria. Gorgas suggested similar tactics could work in Panama.

The Panama Canal project had been difficult from the beginning. The goal was to create a shortcut from the Atlantic Ocean to the Pacific by digging a water-filled path through Panama, the narrowest section of Central America. But immigrants, who had been brought in by a French construction company to dig the canal, were dying by the thousands. From 1881 to 1888, more than five thousand five hundred perished from disease.[9] When the United States bought out the French company in 1904, the United States government sent Gorgas to Panama as a sanitary adviser, even though many people, including President Theodore Roosevelt, still doubted that mosquitoes played a role in spreading diseases. Most still believed filthy and unsanitary conditions were to blame for the epidemics.

41

Gorgas went right to work, using the knowledge he had first gained in Cuba. He sprayed hundreds of pounds of insecticide, spent hundreds of thousands of dollars, and commanded over a thousand laborers. Initially, it appeared his efforts would fail, but after three years, the number of cases of malaria had been cut in half.[10] Gorgas predicted that within a few years, both yellow fever and malaria would be gone. In the end, Dr. William C. Gorgas virtually eliminated both yellow fever and malaria in the canal region. As a result, his work probably contributed more to the completion of the Panama Canal than any of the engineering achievements.

Dr. William Crawford Gorgas, an army major, was sent to clean up the epidemic of yellow fever in Cuba. Later, in 1904, he was sent to Panama, to deal with outbreaks of both yellow fever and malaria. This photo shows him at the Panama Canal project.

The Panama Canal

The Isthmus of Panama was used as a route of travel as early as 8000 B.C., when prehistoric humans moved through Central America to settle in South America. The Spanish began to settle in the area in 1510. They paved mule trails with cobblestones to make travel easier, but building a canal was beyond their abilities. In 1850, developers from the United States began construction of a railroad, to take miners arriving by boat from the east coast of the United States to the gold fields of California. Ships dropped these pioneers on the east coast of Panama, where they traveled by train to ships waiting on the west coast. This shuttle eliminated the long trip around South America and was easier than traveling through the mosquito-ridden area on mules.

In 1880, Ferdinand de Lesseps, who had successfully built the Suez Canal in the Middle East, sold stock to millions of French citizens to raise money to build a canal in Panama. The massive losses of workers from mosquito-borne diseases and other problems led to financial ruin. After Panama became independent from Columbia in 1903, the United States purchased the rights and equipment from his French company, Canal Interocéanique, for $40 million. Ten years, seventy-five thousand men and women, and nearly $400 million later, the Panama Canal opened on August 15, 1914.[11]

4

Yellow Fever

Historical documents that are approximately four hundred years old describe a disease that doctors recognize as yellow fever. It spread to the Americas with the slave trade. Mosquitoes traveled aboard ships, breeding in barrels of water and feeding on the human cargo. In America, yellow fever epidemics swept through both the native populations and the European settlements, killing people by the thousands.

When France sent thirty-three thousand men to conquer Haiti and occupy the Mississippi Valley in 1802, yellow fever killed twenty-nine thousand of them. As a result, France was only too happy to unload the disease-ridden Louisiana Territory to the United States at a bargain price in 1803.[1]

Yellow fever is spread by several kinds of mosquito. Both monkeys and humans can become infected. The cause is a virus that belongs to the *Flavivirus* group. Mosquitoes pick up the virus as they bite. The yellow fever virus multiplies in great quantities inside the mosquito and is then passed on when the mosquito bites another person. Up until the early 1900s, yellow fever outbreaks occurred in Europe and North America as well as in other parts of the world. Now, the disease occurs primarily within an area along the equator in Africa, South America, and the Caribbean Islands. Currently, there are an estimated two hundred thousand cases of yellow fever a year, resulting in thirty thousand deaths.[2]

Yellow fever continues to threaten populated areas. As recently as January 2000, officials in Rio de Janeiro, Brazil, worked to prevent the spread of the disease, after four suspected cases appeared. It was the first time yellow fever had been found in the city since 1942, even though the disease is an ongoing problem in the wilderness areas in the north and central west regions of the country, where it circulates among native animals (mainly monkeys). Across Brazil, sixty-seven people contracted yellow fever in 1999, and twenty-three of them died, nearly double the number of cases from only a year before.[3]

Diagnosis and Treatment

At first, patients infected with yellow fever have no symptoms at all. Then, suddenly, they get a high fever and their pulse rate, or the speed of their heartbeat, drops. They may experience nausea, vomiting, headache, muscle pains, and become extremely tired. These symptoms improve in a few days. If it is a mild case, the patient will return to normal and

In January 2000, for the first time since 1942, suspected cases of yellow fever were found in the city of Rio de Janeiro, Brazil.

be immune from yellow fever in the future. However, in about 15 percent of the cases, the fever and low pulse will return, and patients will enter a "toxic" phase. Patients then develop jaundice. This is a yellowing of the skin that indicates that the liver is not working properly. This symptom is the one that led to the name "yellow fever." Patients may begin to bleed from the mouth, nose, eyes, or stomach. When this happens, they begin to vomit blood. (People in the 1700s called the disease "black vomit.") In the final stages, patients may become delirious or fall into a coma, a very deep sleep. Death often follows. About half of the patients who enter the toxic phase recover.[4] Those who survive will be immune to the yellow fever virus in the future.

There are several ways doctors can diagnose yellow fever. The combination of a slow pulse rate and a high fever is the first sign. If the person has visited a tropical area recently, this combination of symptoms may be enough to make the doctor suspicious. Symptoms such as jaundice and vomiting of blood also point to yellow fever. Doctors can use standard laboratory tests to detect abnormally high levels of protein in the urine and low numbers of white cells in the blood, both of which are common with yellow fever. In addition, a blood test can detect antibodies, or substances the body produces to fight infection, specific to yellow fever. If these are present, they indicate that the patient had been exposed to yellow fever. Specially trained laboratory workers can positively identify the virus from a specimen of the patient's blood. If the patient has died, technicians can examine the patient's liver tissue to make a positive diagnosis.

There is no cure for yellow fever. Doctors place patients on complete bed rest and treat the symptoms of the disease. They give patients medications to reduce vomiting, stop headache pain, and lower fever. Some patients need transfusions to replace blood they have lost through internal bleeding. Doctors also prescribe intravenous solutions (liquids put into the body by a tube in a vein) to replace fluids and correct the body's chemistry. Antibiotics act on bacteria, not viruses, so they help only if the patient has developed a bacterial infection in addition to the yellow fever.

Prognosis

About half of the yellow fever patients who enter the toxic phase die within ten to fourteen days.[5] Death rates are highest among those who get no medical treatment, because it is critical that the patients get enough fluids, a difficult goal without intravenous equipment.

Yellow fever is one of the few mosquito-borne diseases that can be effectively prevented though vaccination. South African microbiologist Max Theiler first developed a vaccine for yellow fever in 1930. Most countries affected by the disease require travelers to be vaccinated before entering the country. The vaccine is safe, effective, and has been in use for several decades. It provides protection for ten years or more. More than 300 million doses of yellow fever vaccine have been given. Serious side effects are rare and occur mostly in children less than six months old, so the vaccine is not given to children that young.[6] Due to the success of the vaccine, yellow fever has been less of a problem in recent years than malaria.

Specially trained laboratory researchers can positively identify the *Flavivirus* that causes yellow fever from a specimen of the patient's blood.

5

Malaria

Ten-year-old Le Ngoc Giang, who lives in Vietnam, is pretty sure he has malaria again. It is the third time this year, so he knows the symptoms well. "I get very tired and begin vomiting," he says. He and his eight-year-old brother walk to the Binh Khanh village clinic. They know the routine. Le Ngoc goes first, stepping up to the nurse, pinching the tip of his finger with the nail of his thumb, so she can prick his finger and squeeze a few drops of blood onto a microscope slide to be analyzed by technicians. His brother goes next. In less than an hour, they have the news. They both have malaria.[1]

Today, people in the United States do not worry much about malaria. But one hundred years ago it was common in New York and New Jersey. As recently as the 1930s, 6 to 7 million Americans a year caught it.[2]

In 1940, malaria was the leading cause of sickness and death around the world.[3] Even now, nearly 300 million people are made sick each year, and over one million people a year die.[4] In Africa, malaria kills more people than any other disease except AIDS.[5]

The parasites that cause malaria are tiny one-celled animals known as protozoans, and are classified within the group called *Plasmodium.* They are *Plasmodium vivax, Plasmodium falciparum, Plasmodium ovale,* and *Plasmodium malariae.* These parasites are smaller than bacteria. They do their damage by sending out merozoites, tiny infectious organisms, which invade a person's red blood cells and begin dividing.

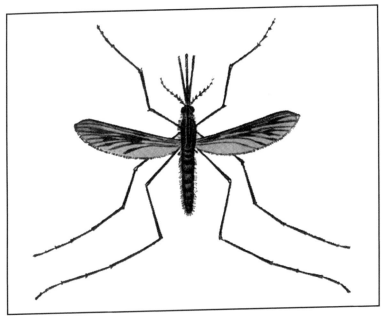

Anopheles quadrimaculatus is the chief malaria vector in the eastern part of the United States.

This process is what causes the cycles of fevers and chills that malaria patients suffer. Malaria parasites can settle in the liver, periodically sending out waves of merozoites, which cause malaria symptoms to come back, even after the patient seems to have recovered. A severe, often fatal, form of malaria is caused by *Plasmodium falciparum*. The *Plasmodium* parasites that cause malaria are spread by mosquitoes of the *Anopheles* species.

When someone gets measles or chicken pox, the immune system, the body's natural means of battling germs and other outside invaders, develops full resistance to the disease. Afterward, the person will never get that disease again. Unfortunately, malaria does not create the same response. Someone who has had malaria may have a small amount of protective immunity, but it is not enough to prevent the person from getting malaria again, or from carrying the malaria parasites for lengthy periods of time. This is why malaria kills millions of people every year. Adults who survived malaria as children can become carriers. When mosquitoes bite them, the insects pick up the malaria parasite and pass it on to infants or others who have never had the disease.

Incidence

In the past fifteen years, nearly 50 million people worldwide have died of malaria. By comparison, during the same period, 5 million died of AIDS.[6] One child dies from malaria every thirty seconds.[7] Compare these figures to the well-publicized Ebola outbreak that triggered books, movies, and widespread

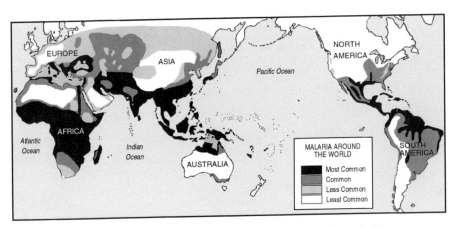

Malaria is most common in tropical and certain subtropical areas, including New Delhi, India, and some parts of South Africa.

fear. The total number of people who died from Ebola in all of the outbreaks combined was less than a thousand.

The geographic areas at risk for malaria have shrunk considerably over the past fifty years through aggressive prevention programs, but the disease is still a major problem in Africa, parts of South America, and Southeast Asia. In addition, malaria is re-emerging in areas where it had previously been under control. The World Wide Fund for Nature, an international environmental organization that is known in the United States as the World Wildlife Fund, predicts that the most dangerous strain, *Plasmodium falciparum*, could soon reach southern Europe.

In the United States, most cases of malaria are in people who got infected while overseas. Yet there are about ten cases of malaria a year in people who got infected in the United

States. In 1999, two boy scouts camping on Long Island not far from New York City were infected with malaria.[8]

Some people of African heritage have a natural immunity to malaria. Slave traders first noticed this fact, and since that time scientists have tried to find out why. At first, the secret to immunity seemed to be eating a lot of yams, a vegetable similar to the sweet potato. Then scientists noticed that the areas in West Africa where yams are grown are also areas where many people carry a genetic characteristic called the sickle cell trait. When a child inherits the sickle cell trait from both parents, he or she develops sickle cell anemia, a painful disease that causes early death. However, inheriting the trait from just one parent makes people partially immune to malaria. They may get sick from malaria, but it is not likely that they will die.

It turns out that over the years, farmers in West Africa slashed down trees and burned them to clear land to plant

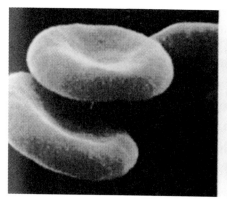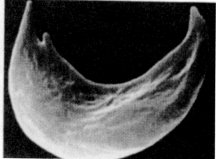

Normal red blood cells (left) are doughnut shaped. However, with sickle cell anemia, the red blood cells (right) become sickle shaped (hence the name of the disease).

yams. The trees had provided sheltered areas where water could collect, giving mosquitoes places to breed. The trees also provided a habitat for animals that mosquitoes could use as sources of blood. Once the trees were gone, malaria-carrying mosquitoes moved on, searching for new areas. This often brought them into more populated areas, where they infected humans. The sickle cell trait may be a natural genetic adaptation that protected people living in areas that had long-term exposure to malaria.[9]

Diagnosis and Treatment

After a malaria-infected mosquito bites, it can take as short a period as six to eight days or as long as several months until the victim develops symptoms. By the time symptoms appear, the person may not even remember the mosquito bite, much less connect it with their illness. This time lapse between cause and effect is one reason it took scientists so long to realize that mosquitoes were the carriers of the disease.

Patients with malaria suffer symptoms similar to those of influenza, or "the flu." They may have aches, feelings of weakness, and vomiting. Their spleen and liver may become enlarged. The most common symptoms are fever and chills. Some patients have fever and chills but no other symptoms. The fever and chills go away, but they can come back, often several times. The length of any particular bout and the time between bouts depend upon the particular type of malaria parasite involved.

The most dangerous form of malaria is that caused by *Plasmodium falciparum*. Patients infected with this parasite can develop a complication known as cerebral malaria. Patients run a fever of 104 degrees or higher, become delirious, and may develop hemorrhages (bleeding) in the brain. This can lead to coma and, eventually, death. This form of the disease is most commonly seen in infants, pregnant women, and travelers who have never been exposed to malaria.

The pattern of being sick and then seeming to recover makes malaria hard to diagnose. Doctors in the United States, unused to seeing cases of malaria, generally suspect influenza or some other virus instead. But when symptoms have disappeared and then keep coming back, doctors will generally look further. An ultrasound test (a procedure that uses sound waves to create images of internal body structures) can reveal an enlarged spleen, one common sign of the disease. However, a blood test is the only way to positively diagnose the disease. The doctor takes a sample of blood from the patient and sends it to a laboratory. There, the blood is smeared onto a glass slide and examined under a microscope to see whether any of the four parasites that cause human malaria is present.

The oldest treatment for malaria is quinine. Unfortunately, this medicine is expensive, must be given in large doses for long periods of time, and causes side effects such as ringing ears, fever, and allergic reactions. These problems led scientists to develop a new drug, chloraquine. It is similar to quinine in structure, but safer and less expensive. Both drugs treat malaria by preventing the invading parasite from sending out merozoites, which invade the red blood cells and cause the symptoms of disease. For malaria caused by two types of parasites, *Plasmodium falciparum* and *Plasmodium malariae,* the effect of the drugs is enough to cure the disease. For malaria caused by others, these drugs will treat only the initial attack.

By the 1950s, more people worldwide were taking chloraquine than any other drug except aspirin.[10] But over the years, the malaria parasite became resistant to chloraquine, and the treatment became much less effective. Scientists struggled to find new antimalaria treatments.

Doctors often combine drugs to help reduce the chances that the malaria parasite will become resistant to a single medication. Newer treatments include a combination of two

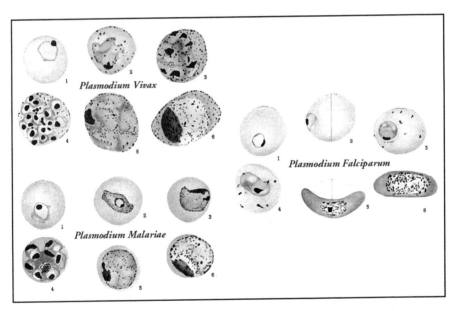

These diagrams show blood smears under the microscope for three important human strains of malaria.

drugs, chlorproguanil and dapsone, for patients who do not have a severe form of malaria and are otherwise healthy. This drug combination was developed through a team effort involving the World Bank, the World Health Organization, the SmithKline Beecham pharmaceutical company, and other organizations. Another new drug is artesunate, a suppository (a pill that is inserted into the rectum). This medication helps those who are vomiting repeatedly. It works quickly and can help buy time for people in remote areas who must make a long trip to get to a hospital, where they can then be given injections or intravenous treatments.

Scientists are also working to uncover the genetic code of the malaria parasite. In November 1999, scientists at the National Institute of Allergy and Infectious Diseases in Bethesda, Maryland, produced the first detailed genetic map of *Plasmodium falciparum*, the deadliest of the malaria parasites. The map will help scientists locate genes in the parasite that make it resistant to drugs and that cause the severe malarial symptoms.[11] Knowing how the organism's genes work may also help scientists develop more effective drugs.

In 2000, scientists in Australia finally discovered how the malaria parasite has been able to become resistant to drugs. They found that a protein called Pgh1 is involved in changes in a gene. These genetic changes in the parasite prevent certain drugs from accumulating in the parasites' cell. The altered gene either stops the antimalarial drugs from entering the parasite's cell or rapidly pumps them out. This knowledge may help scientists develop a way to reverse the process and allow the drugs to enter and remain in the parasites' cells. Unlocking that mystery would make existing drugs effective again.[12]

Prognosis

Patients with malaria caused by the milder parasites usually improve, even without treatment, in ten to thirty days. However, their symptoms can come back time after time. Children under age five in Africa often have chronic (long-lasting) cases and may suffer six or more bouts a year. Patients infected with the *falciparum* parasite may develop cerebral malaria, a dangerous complication. In this type, the capillaries in the brain become blocked, and the person often dies.

Scientists have had difficulty developing a vaccine for malaria. They face some of the same problems that prevent the immune system from developing full immunity to malaria. For example, the parasite that causes malaria gets inside red blood cells, where the immune system cannot work. Even antibodies, infection-fighting substances produced by the body or introduced by vaccination, cannot get at the parasites when they are inside the red blood cells. In addition, the malaria parasite goes through many stages, during which it keeps changing its identity, making it even harder to attack. Another problem is that parasites of the same species but from other geographic locations can be different enough that a vaccine that protects against one may not work against another. The genetic structure of the malaria parasite is also complex. Each parasite has a thousand times as many genes as the HIV virus that causes AIDS.[13]

Most vaccine research efforts have concentrated on the *Plasmodium falciparum* parasite because it causes the most severe form of the disease. Some experimental vaccines target specific stages of development of the malaria parasite, but each of these has limitations. For example, a vaccine that protects against the infectious form of the malaria parasite would only be useful for travelers or others who are exposed briefly. This is because it attacks only parasites in an early stage of development. If a single organism survived to develop and reproduce, the person could still develop full-blown malaria. One possible solution would be a vaccine "cocktail" that combined several kinds of vaccines.

Other researchers are looking at the way the parasite prevents the immune system from attacking infected red blood cells. Once they figure out how that process works, the researchers can then develop a method to stop it. Although the development of an effective vaccine for malaria is a challenge, it holds the best hope for conquering this major killer.

6

Other Mosquito-Borne Diseases

West Nile virus, malaria, and yellow fever are only three of the diseases spread by mosquitoes. There are at least eighteen other viruses that are also carried by them.[1] Some are rarely seen or are found only in small areas of the world. Others affect many people across Africa, parts of Asia, Australia, South America, and parts of North America.

Dengue and Rift Valley Fever

Dengue is a disease commonly found in more than one hundred countries in Africa, the Americas, the Eastern Mediterranean, Southeast Asia, and the Western Pacific (Australia, New Zealand, and numerous islands).[2] Dengue fever and dengue hemorrhagic (bleeding) fever are illnesses caused by any of four closely related types of *Flavivirus*, a virus spread by *Aedes* mosquitoes.

The first epidemic of dengue fever was reported in 1779 to 1780. It broke out on three continents: Africa, Asia, and North America. After that time, there were outbreaks every ten to forty years. Then, after World War II, an outbreak started in Southeast Asia that spread around the world.[3] It is still raging.

Over the past forty years, the number of cases of dengue has increased at least twenty times. The World Health Organization estimates that there are now 50 million cases of dengue worldwide each year.[4] The areas at risk for dengue have also increased. In 1998, there were more than six hundred sixteen thousand cases of dengue in the Americas

Which Diseases Are Transmitted by Mosquitoes?

Transmitted by Mosquitoes	NOT Transmitted by Mosquitoes
Dengue Fever	AIDS
Eastern Equine Encephalitis	Ebola
Heartworm	Mad Cow Disease
Malaria	Measles
Rift Valley Fever	Plague
St. Louis Encephalitis	Pneumonia
West Nile Virus	Tuberculosis
Yellow Fever	Rabies

(more than double the number reported just three years earlier).[5] In 1997, an estimated 2.5 billion people lived in areas at risk for a dengue epidemic (about two fifths of the world's population).[6] Many more travel to vacation spots, such as those in South America and the Caribbean, where cases of dengue fever have grown dramatically in the last decade.

Although the disease is still uncommon in the United States, the number of cases of dengue fever rose in 1998. There were ninety confirmed cases (many among people who had traveled to areas where dengue fever is more common). At

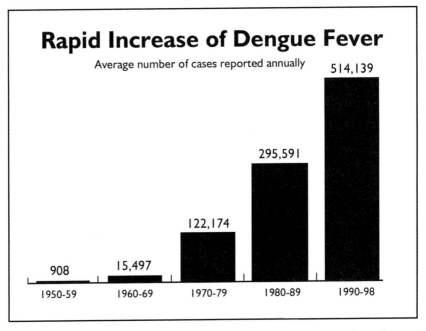

Rapid Increase of Dengue Fever

Average number of cases reported annually

1950-59	1960-69	1970-79	1980-89	1990-98
908	15,497	122,174	295,591	514,139

Over the past forty years, the number of cases of dengue fever has increased at least twenty times. In 2000, the World Health Organization estimated that there are about 50 million cases worldwide each year.

least seven people were hospitalized and one died of the disease. This was a 70 percent increase over the year before.[7]

Dengue diseases can cause anything from a mild viral illness to a severe or fatal hemorrhage. Patients with dengue fever often have the obvious fever, plus a rash, headache, and the severe pains in the joints and muscles that once led to its early name, "breakbone fever." Dengue fever can be diagnosed by a blood test. There is no cure, only treatment for its symptoms, which usually go away in about a week. It is rarely fatal.

Patients with dengue hemorrhagic fever suffer from fever, headache, vomiting, and a cough. The most severe symptom, however, is excessive bleeding. Without treatment, 20 percent or more of the patients may die. With hospitalization, which provides medical supervision and assures replacement of lost body fluids through intravenous treatments, this rate can be reduced to less than one percent.[8]

Rift Valley fever was first found among livestock in Kenya in the early 1900s. It is still most common in livestock, but now it affects humans in Africa as well as cattle, sheep, camels, and goats there. It is caused by a virus in the *Phlebovirus* group. The *Aedes* mosquito carries Rift Valley virus only to livestock. Female *Aedes* mosquitoes can pass the virus to their eggs, so when the mosquitoes hatch they are already infected. *Culex* mosquitoes can bite infected livestock and then carry the disease to humans. Outbreaks of Rift Valley fever often follow heavy rains, which trigger massive mosquito hatches. Rift Valley fever is also spread through human contact with

Rift Valley fever is found among livestock such as cattle, sheep, camels, and goats.

the body fluids or organs of infected animals, as well as through mosquito bites.

Rift Valley fever is usually mild, with symptoms such as fever, headache, muscle pain, and sometimes neck stiffness or sensitivity to light. In some cases, patients may develop problems that can lead to damaged vision, hemorrhaging, or inflammation of the brain. However, less than one percent of infected people die.[9]

Doctors use blood tests to diagnose Rift Valley fever. There is no treatment as yet, but ribavirin, an antiviral drug, has shown promise for the future.[10]

Encephalitis and Others

There are also several types of encephalitis that can be spread by mosquitoes. They differ in severity. St. Louis encephalitis has a fatality rate of 10 percent or less, while the eastern equine encephalitis kills half of its human victims.[11]

Other, less common mosquito-borne diseases include Barmah Forest virus, found only in Australia, which causes outbreaks of polyarthritis (inflammation of several joints at once) in humans. Ross River virus, a similar mosquito-borne disease, is also found in Australia. Mosquitoes can also carry *Wuchereria bancrofti*, a tiny worm that causes elephantiasis, a disease that causes massive swelling. It was Patrick Manson's observation of this phenomenon in 1877 that resulted in the first realization that mosquitoes can spread disease.

Even relatively unknown mosquito-borne diseases may play a larger role in human health issues than had previously been thought. For example, a 1996 Colorado State University study suggested that pregnant women exposed to viruses such as the Cache Valley or Tensaw varieties (which are carried by mosquitoes) may have a greater chance of delivering babies with central nervous system problems.[12] Dr. Bruce Harrison, a medical entomologist with the North Carolina Department of Environment, Health, and Natural Resources, said: "There are a lot more viruses out there and not all of them are as harmless as we thought."[13]

Experts agree that no matter what becomes of the West Nile virus in North America, there will continue to be outbreaks of mosquito-borne diseases in new areas. Public health officials are continuing to develop plans for responding to such unexpected outbreaks.

7

Animals and Mosquito-Borne Diseases

Humans are not the only animals troubled by mosquito-borne illnesses. Diseases such as Rift Valley fever, encephalitis, and malaria affect a variety of animals. Malaria affects birds, rodents, monkeys, and even snakes, although the animal forms of the disease are caused by different parasites than the ones that cause the human form. The tree hole mosquito that carries LaCrosse encephalitis lives in woodland habitats where it spreads the disease among squirrels and chipmunks. Birds are common victims of mosquito-borne diseases. And one of the most common problems affecting family pets—heartworm—is spread by mosquitoes. Heartworms are worms that live in the heart and in the large blood vessels of the lungs of infected animals. They can cause death if not stopped.

Threats to Farm Animals

Outbreaks of mosquito-borne diseases can have a devastating effect on farm animals and other forms of wildlife. The loss of farm animals, however, is especially critical because in many areas people depend upon these animals as sources of food or income. "Outbreaks can have a profound economic impact on agriculture," said Dr. David Durrheim, a communicable disease control consultant called in during an outbreak of Rift Valley fever in 1998–1999 in Mpumalanga, Africa.[1] Rift Valley virus is a disease that primarily affects cattle, sheep, buffalo, camels, and goats. A single outbreak in East Africa in 1998 killed 70 percent of the sheep and goats and 20 to 30 percent of the cattle and camels.[2]

When there are many deer or horses around, mosquitoes have plenty of blood sources, and bite humans at a lower rate. Some scientists think that the growth of deer populations (in North Carolina, the number of deer rose from twenty thousand in 1920 to nine hundred thousand in 1996), has helped reduce the number of human outbreaks.

Eastern equine encephalitis is one of many mosquito-borne diseases that affect animals other than humans. It is known as "equine" (relating to horses) because the presence of dead horses is sometimes the first sign that this disease is spreading. However, horses are dead-end hosts for this primarily bird-and-mosquito-cycled disease. Horses do not produce enough of the virus in their blood to be taken up by a previously uninfected mosquito, so they never pass the disease on to other animals.

Eastern equine encephalitis and West Nile virus can be deadly for horses. They get both diseases from mosquito bites.

Horses also get West Nile virus, which kills 40 percent of the horses it infects.[3] As New York faced its first outbreak of West Nile virus in 1999, foreign countries became concerned. Officials in Hong Kong temporarily halted the import of horses from North America. They feared the horses might be infected with the disease. Not only were the officials concerned about the disease affecting their own horses, but they worried that the virus could spread within the local mosquito population and begin transmission to birds, other animals, and people.[4]

The West Nile virus hit birds the hardest. According to one estimate, as many as two thirds of the crows in and around

New York City may have died in the 1999 outbreak.[5] But the disease also killed birds from at least twenty other species, including robins, rock doves, hawks, blue jays, and bald eagles.

One way researchers can monitor the spread of the disease is by keeping small flocks of chickens (groups of three to five birds) and testing their blood frequently. This monitoring system can serve as an early warning alarm and is more efficient than simply searching for dead crows. To check for the spread of West Nile virus, flocks of such monitored chickens are being kept in suburban New Jersey, New York, and Connecticut locations, as well as in New York City.[6]

The 1999 outbreak of West Nile virus in the New York area killed many birds, including crows, robins, hawks, blue jays, and bald eagles.

Diagnosis and Treatment

Livestock are kept in herds. Unlike family pets, individual animals are not usually examined unless a health problem becomes obvious. Therefore, the first sign of an outbreak may be that several animals are dead. A positive diagnosis is often made by conducting an autopsy, or a dissection and analysis of a dead animal's tissues, to determine the cause of death.

In some cases, blood tests are used to see whether living animals have been exposed to a particular disease. This kind of testing can be used to determine whether it is safe to import animals from areas where outbreaks have occurred. (The animals are not shipped unless blood tests prove they have not been infected.)

There are animal vaccines available for some diseases, such as Rift Valley fever and equine encephalitis. If an outbreak is confirmed, animals can be vaccinated, which will help each animal fight off the disease. But even vaccination does not prevent the loss of livestock. In Florida, for example, even with a widespread vaccination program, about one hundred fifty horses die each year from eastern equine encephalitis.[7]

In the case of Rift Valley fever, new satellite data that scientists can use to predict weather patterns will help provide a two- to five-month warning period. If the weather patterns show that conditions will favor a large mosquito hatch (which would likely lead to a disease outbreak), people can be given a warning in time to vaccinate their livestock.

Heartworm

If you have a dog, your veterinarian has probably drawn its blood to test for heartworm. Heartworms are worms visible to the eye (they can grow to be over a foot long) that live in the heart and large blood vessels of the lungs of infected dogs. They cause coughing, weakness, shortness of breath, heart failure, and, if untreated, death.

Adult heartworms produce tiny organisms called microfilariae that circulate in the blood of an infected dog. A mosquito that bites a dog with heartworms takes up these microfilariae with the blood meal. These tiny organisms grow,

Heartworm in dogs can be deadly, as the worms multiply and block vital pathways in the dog's body.

71

developing into an infective stage. They spread inside the mosquito, eventually reaching the mosquito's mouthparts. As the mosquito bites another animal, it injects the infective microfilariae into the new host while taking a blood meal. Heartworms that enter hosts other than dogs usually die within a few days.

The life cycle of the heartworm depends upon the mosquito. Microfilariae cannot develop into adults without passing through the body of a female mosquito. They mature inside the mosquito's digestive tract before they are passed on to an animal to grow into adult worms. Heartworm also affects foxes, wolves, and cats, but is most common in dogs.

It is much easier to prevent heartworm in dogs than to treat it. There are a variety of drugs pet owners can use routinely to prevent their dogs from ever becoming infected. These medications are usually given once a month during mosquito season (spring through fall), in the form of a chewable pill. Chemicals in the drug will kill the microfilariae injected by the mosquito before they can move into the animal's organs and cause damage.

Once a dog has heartworm, medications can be given to kill both the adult worms and the microfilariae. This can be a dangerous process, however. First, the veterinarian gives injections to kill the adult heartworms. There is usually a series of four injections given over a period of two days. As the heartworms die and break up, they can form clots that block the animal's organs. It can take a month for the animal to recover completely. After this period, the veterinarian can give a second medication to kill the microfilariae. This medication can also take its toll on the animal, causing vomiting, loss of appetite, and drooling. If heartworm infection is not identified and treated, it can cause severe bleeding, heart damage, liver disorders, and eventually kill the animal.

Although it is not as common, heartworm can also be transmitted to cats by mosquitoes. Blood tests can detect heartworm in cats, but the accuracy of the test depends upon the number of worms present. Sometimes X rays or ultrasound, another imaging technique, can help veterinarians find heartworm in cats. According to veterinarian Rich Brtva, "They appear like railroad tracks across a cat's heart."[8] Cats almost always host fewer worms than dogs, making diagnosis more difficult.

Heartworm treatment can be even more hazardous for cats than for dogs. Since cats have smaller arteries than most dogs, it is easier for the circulating pieces of worm to get stuck and block the blood flow to critical organs. For this reason, prevention is best. Veterinarian David Knight, a professor of cardiology at the University of Pennsylvania, estimates that 10 percent of dogs have heartworm, and 1 or 2 percent of cats have it. There are now medications designed especially for preventing heartworm in cats.[9] These work in the same way as the treatments for dogs.

8

Mosquito-Borne Diseases and Society

Considering its tiny size, the mosquito has proved to be a very large troublemaker. The price society has paid for mosquito-borne diseases is so great that it is difficult to add up. Beyond the millions of lives lost, there are personal and financial hardships suffered by families with someone who has a mosquito-borne illness. And there are extreme economic costs to the struggling countries where many of the victims live. Add to these factors the damage to the environment and human health caused by the massive use of toxic pesticides in the battle against mosquitoes. Even the price of fear must be added in, as people avoid outdoor activities in the evening, change vacation plans, and worry about episodes of pesticide spraying during mosquito-borne disease outbreaks.

A Growing World

In 1899, there were 1.5 billion people on earth. One hundred years later, that number had jumped to over 6 billion.[1] Not only is the world population exploding, it is growing fastest in the parts of the world where mosquito-borne diseases are common and where medical and public health resources are least available. The United Nations estimates that by the year

Mortality rates are high in city slums of many underdeveloped countries, where residents are crowded and conditions are often unsanitary.

2015, twenty-two of the twenty-six largest cities on the planet will be located in underdeveloped regions. These huge cities will include Bombay, India (26 million people by 2015); Lagos, Nigeria (24 million); Dhaka, Bangladesh (19 million); and Karachi, Pakistan (19 million).[2] The growth of large cities in tropical areas, experts say, will make the war against mosquito-borne diseases even more difficult. When huge numbers of people are packed into tight urban areas, particularly in areas with poor sanitation, epidemics become a major threat. As rainforests are destroyed, mosquitoes look for new homes. And as world trade and international passenger traffic increases, there are more chances for mosquitoes to hitch rides and move into new areas.

The Financial Side

Mosquito-borne diseases are extremely costly. Some of these diseases kill millions of cattle and other food animals, reducing the amount of meat that can be sold. Governments struggle with the costs of reducing mosquito populations, providing vaccinations to the public, and controlling disease outbreaks. Governments and private industry lose many days of labor due to sick employees.

In 1997, the estimated cost of malaria alone (health expenses, production losses due to sick workers, and the strain on the medical system) in sub-Saharan Africa was $2 billion.[3] Costs to individual families include lost wages and the price of prevention and treatment. The countries hit hardest by malaria and other mosquito-borne diseases are also the

As world trade and international passenger traffic increase, there are more chances for mosquitoes to hitch rides and move into new areas.

poorest. These are the ones that can least afford expensive vaccines, public health programs, efforts to educate the population, and treatments.

These diseases can also lead to additional problems, which may cost money down the road. Children may miss school and fall behind. Malaria can drain important nutrients from their bodies, slowing their mental or physical growth. Sick parents cannot properly care for their children. Malaria is particularly dangerous to pregnant women. It causes severe anemia, a condition that reduces the amount of oxygen the blood can carry, weakening the body. Women who have malaria in addition to the HIV virus are more likely to die during childbirth and have a higher chance of passing the HIV virus to their babies.

In farming communities, an outbreak of malaria would mean that farmers could not tend their crops at critical times, and therefore would not be able to make the amount of money they depend on for the year. Malaria outbreaks are often at their peak during harvest time. Young adults, who are often hit hard during these outbreaks, may miss as many as ten working days from a single bout. Their loss of wages makes poor families even poorer. In addition, experts estimate that farmers in Nigeria, for example, spend as much as 13 percent of their family's household budget on malaria treatments.[4]

The estimated average cost of discovering, testing, and releasing a new drug is $500 million. American pharmaceutical companies have not been interested in spending that much money for a drug needed mainly in countries where most people cannot afford it. For this reason, governments and charitable foundations have created special programs to encourage new drug development.

Disease Control vs. Environmental Protection

In the past, people have regarded wetlands as swamps that should be drained, both to rid them of mosquitoes and to provide land for other uses. Until recent years, a half million acres of wetlands were being destroyed every year. Now, scientists realize that wetland habitats are important to the environment. They help reduce flooding, filter and clean water, and provide habitats for many species of animals. As a result, it has become more important to find ways to control mosquitoes rather than to simply destroy wetlands. According to Robert Gwadz of the National Institute of Allergy and Infectious Diseases' Laboratory of Parasitic Diseases in Bethesda, Maryland, "What we need is to strike a balance."[5]

In December 1999, people protested work being done to clear trees and drain water from the Salt River bed that lies west of the Tempe Town Lake in Arizona. The area, popular among hikers, was a prime breeding area for mosquitoes, some of which had been shown to carry the western equine encephalitis virus. But the area was also a natural area with cottonwood trees, salt cedars, and lush vegetation. County officials weighed the value of the habitat against the potential risk of disease to the neighboring community. They removed only trees that were not native to the area. Then they took away only the amount of dirt and plants necessary to allow water to drain from the river bottom.[6]

As mosquito-borne diseases become more of a threat, particularly in previously untroubled areas, communities increasingly will have to make compromises between protecting habitats and eliminating mosquito breeding grounds.

9

Prevention

It is always better to prevent a disease than to have to treat it. This is particularly true in the case of mosquito-borne diseases. If infected mosquitoes can be killed, kept from biting new hosts, and/or prevented from picking up disease-causing organisms in the first place, the cycle of transmission can be broken. If people can be vaccinated to prevent them from getting the disease, lives can be saved. Scientists and public health officials are working with every weapon and piece of knowledge they have to prevent the spread of mosquito-borne diseases.

Vaccines

Scientists credit vaccines with wiping out smallpox and nearly eliminating polio. As a result, finding vaccines for the major mosquito-borne diseases has been a prime focus of health researchers. Malaria has been the most difficult challenge.

Since the mid-1970s, scientists have known a way to protect people from malaria for about six months. They take mosquitoes that carry the *Plasmodium falciparum* parasite and irradiate them, or treat them with a dose of radiation. Then they allow the irradiated mosquitoes to bite people. This technique works like a vaccination. People who are bitten by the irradiated mosquitoes develop a weak form of malaria that prevents them from getting a full-blown case. Malaria parasites from irradiated mosquitoes can reach the liver of the host but cannot get to the red blood cells, where they would start to trigger the symptoms of malaria. These parasites cause the body to produce antibodies to malaria for a period of about six months. Scientists are now working on a vaccine that mimics this irradiation effect.

Researchers at the Walter Reed Army Institute in Washington, D.C., are developing a vaccine that fools the body into thinking that malaria parasites are bursting from the liver to infect red blood cells. This makes the body's immune system produce antibodies to fight malaria. If the vaccinated person is then exposed to live malaria parasites, the person's antibodies will attack them.[1] Another group of scientists, at the Naval Medical Research Center in Bethesda, Maryland, are using parts of genes from the malaria parasite to cause the same kind of immune response.[2]

In 1999, computer software pioneer Bill Gates donated $50 million toward the development of a vaccine for malaria.

A nonprofit organization called the Program for Appropriate Technology in Health, located in Seattle, Washington, launched the Malaria Vaccine Initiative. Its goal is to use Gates's donation to fund the most promising research projects.

Despite the money being spent, creating a safe, inexpensive, easy-to-use vaccine that provides lifelong protection against malaria will be tricky. No effective vaccine has ever been developed for a parasite (most vaccines are for viruses). "If everything goes well for the leading candidates, there could be a vaccine available in the next fifteen years," says Dr. Howard Engers of the World Health Organization's vaccination development program. "But it would be a mistake to be overly optimistic," he points out.[3]

A vaccine for dengue fever is under development but is not currently available. It is difficult to immunize patients for dengue because it is caused by any of four different viruses, and protection against only one or two of them might actually increase the risk of serious disease. Vaccines for Rift Valley fever can successfully prevent the disease in animals, but researchers are still experimenting with a vaccine for humans. Yellow fever is the only common mosquito-borne disease for which a safe and effective vaccine for humans exists.

Killing or Repelling Mosquitoes

Once Ronald Ross discovered that mosquitoes carried malaria, the solution seemed obvious: kill the mosquitoes. Thus began a worldwide battle.

In 1874, Viennese pharmacist Othmar Ziedler invented the chemical compound that became the world's most powerful weapon for killing mosquitoes: dichlorodiphenyl trichloroethane, or DDT. But DDT's value went unnoticed for more than sixty years. During World War II, Paul Muller, a Swiss citizen working for a chemical company, rediscovered the formula while looking for a substance to control clothing moths. He gave some of the formula to the United States Army, whose personnel had been facing thousands of casualties due to mosquito-borne diseases when fighting in tropical areas. The army found it was just what they had been looking for: a substance that was cheap to make and could wipe out large mosquito populations. DDT was so powerful that surfaces sprayed with it still killed mosquitoes that landed on them months later.[4]

The World Health Organization came up with a plan. They would spray DDT on every wall of every building in every place in the world at risk for malaria twice a year for five years. Early tests performed in the Tennessee River Valley and other areas were great successes. The scientists believed that by following their plan, they could wipe out malaria. The Global Eradication of Malaria Program, begun in 1955, would be costly. Nevertheless, scientists were convinced it could succeed.

The plan was to make malaria extinct by the 1990s. It nearly worked. In India, cases of malaria dropped from an estimated 75 million in 1951 to just fifty thousand in 1961.[5] All over the world, the incidence of malaria was dramatically reduced. But by 1969 scientists realized they were losing the battle. Mosquitoes were becoming resistant to DDT. They simply moved outdoors, never landing on the insecticide-sprayed walls. Some species of mosquitoes were so efficient they could pick up and pass on malaria before the DDT killed them. Scientists scrambled to develop new insecticides, but they were much more expensive, and few countries could afford them. That is why the United States is one of the few regions that continues to be nearly free of malaria. In Florida alone, the government spends $300 million a year on mosquito control (draining swamps, spraying, trapping and testing, applying chemicals and oils to bodies of water, etc.).[6]

Some people say that DDT caused more problems than it solved. Although the National Academy of Sciences called it the greatest chemical ever discovered, and experts say it saved an estimated 500 million lives, DDT is now banned in the United States and in thirty-three other countries.[7] A number of organizations, including the World Wildlife Fund, Physicians for Social Responsibility, and the International Organization of Consumer Unions, want to see it banned around the world. "DDT is such a potent chemical that as long as it is used anywhere in the world, nobody is safe," says Clifton Curtis, director of the World Wildlife Fund's Global Toxics Initiative.[8]

The World Wildlife Fund maintains that DDT can travel thousands of miles in the air, water, or through the food chain, resulting in global contamination. It claims that even minor exposure to DDT can cause cancer and disrupt production of human hormones. In addition, the body cannot break down

DDT. As a result, DDT accumulates in body fat. It can also end up in human breast milk. According to the United States Agency for Toxic Substances and Disease Registry, DDT was found in soil seventeen years after its use was banned. Experts continue to argue over whether DDT is harmful to humans (the evidence is not firm).[9]

DDT has also been blamed for the deaths of animals, especially birds. Several species of birds (peregrine falcons, brown pelicans, ospreys, and bald eagles) nearly became extinct, at least in part, due to DDT poisoning. In her famous 1962 book, *Silent Spring*, marine biologist Rachel Carson explained how robins died after eating worms that had eaten leaves of Dutch elm trees that had been sprayed with DDT.

Public health officials in other countries argue that the use of DDT is necessary. They claim that a ban would cost the lives of millions of people in poor countries. Industrialized countries have no right, some say, to impose their own environmental standards on countries that cannot afford the increased costs of huge

In *Silent Spring*, published in 1962, Rachel Carson described how robins had died from eating worms whose diet had been contaminated with DDT.

epidemics. "The relevant question," states Dr. Amir Attaran, head of the Malaria Project in Washington, D.C., "is not whether DDT use has some risks (it does), but whether the risks outweigh the . . . public health benefits of malaria control (they do not)."[10]

DDT is not the only insecticide that has worried people. During the West Nile virus outbreak in the New York area, officials sprayed a chemical called malathion over large tracts of land, including areas where people live. The chemical is a widely used pesticide, considered safe by public health officials. Yet some studies have shown that it can damage cells, perhaps causing cancer. Many residents were concerned about its widespread use.

Another problem is that mosquitoes, like other animals, adapt in order to survive. Each time humans come up with a new insecticide for killing mosquitoes, a few are able to resist its effects. These few insecticide-resistant mosquitoes then breed thousands more, and before long the new chemicals are no longer effective. That is why attention has shifted from using more and more insecticides, which ultimately prove ineffective in some species, to other methods of control.

The need to balance a concern for the environment with a concern for both cost-effectiveness and the risks to human health continues. On March 2, 2000, New York State senator Carl Marcellino, whose district includes areas of Long Island that were sprayed during the West Nile outbreak, held a hearing in Huntington to address residents' concerns about insecticide spraying. Angry environmental activists shouted

New York State senator Carl Marcellino examines a map showing areas that were sprayed with insecticide during the 1999 West Nile virus outbreak in and near New York City.

from the audience while health department officials spoke about the 1999 spraying program.

Dominic Ninivaggi, superintendent of the Vector Control Program of the Department of Public Works in Suffolk County spoke at the hearing. He told attendees that while spraying attracts the most attention, it represents only about 10 percent of the department's efforts. Far more important, he maintained, is to kill the larvae before they emerge as adults. This can be done with chemicals that act directly on the larvae, so there is less danger to humans and other wildlife than with sprayed chemicals. Ninivaggi also explained that his department uses biological controls (microbial insecticides that act on mosquitoes but do not affect other wildlife). However, Ninivaggi explained that the control department must use many tools to avoid having the mosquitoes become resistant to any single one.[11]

The activists argued that the chemicals used were far more dangerous than officials had led the public to believe. In a news release distributed at the meeting, Senator Marcellino promised: "If this hearing leads to the conclusion that the spraying endangers the health and welfare of the citizens of Long Island, then I fully intend to develop legislation which will protect them."[12]

Another weapon available in the fight against mosquitoes is chemical repellents that discourage mosquitoes from biting.

These come in the form of sprays, creams, oils, liquids, and solids that people can spread on their skin or clothing. Protection lasts about six hours. People can also use other substances, in other ways. Oil of citronella, for example, when burned in candles, produces a

Dominic Ninivaggi from the Department of Public Works in Suffolk County, New York, speaks at a public hearing about the department's mosquito vector control program.

smoke that repels mosquitoes. This helps clear an outdoor area temporarily so that people can sit outdoors without being bothered by the pests. Although burning citronella is effective over an area wider than one's own personal space (depending upon the wind conditions), it is still less effective than applying repellents directly to the body or clothing.

Companies also sell foggers and other space sprays that knock down mosquitoes within a certain prescribed area. These provide immediate results, but they are only temporary. Outdoors, the sprays disappear quickly, and new mosquitoes soon fly into the area.

In areas with large mosquito populations, commercial spraying is often the only effective solution. In Florida and other states with warm, damp climates that encourage mosquito breeding, mosquito control organizations, government health departments, and private companies offer professional mosquito management. These procedures include draining swampy areas, surveying residential areas, educating residents about mosquito control, and treating breeding areas with ground or aerial spraying. Some local governments have established mosquito management districts in an attempt to organize efforts at reducing the mosquito populations.

Although state and local health departments continue to assure communities that they apply insecticides carefully, many people are concerned about the effects of the chemicals.

Not only may they be hazardous to human health, but chemicals that are poisonous to one type of animal are usually dangerous to others, as well. When Mike Shirley, resource management coordinator for the Rookery Bay National Estuarine Research Reserve in Florida, noticed hundreds of dying fiddler crabs one day in 1992, he suspected they had been poisoned. After finding that the area had been sprayed to control mosquitoes, Shirley knew he had found the answer. If spraying had continued in the same manner, between 80 and 90 percent of the fiddler crabs in the area would have died.[13] Crabs and mosquitoes are close relatives, and react in similar ways to pesticides being used.

To prevent harm to the crabs, scientists developed a spray that produced smaller droplets. Tests showed that misting, rather than traditional spraying, killed more mosquitoes in flight, and less insecticide reached the ground, where it could kill other animals. By discovering ways to use chemicals in a more targeted fashion, scientists are able to minimize their effect on other animals.[14]

One alternative to chemicals is microbial insecticides. Instead of toxic chemicals, these solutions contain microorganisms or substances produced by microorganisms. Microbial insecticides are applied like chemicals: in sprays, dusts, or granules. They contain viruses, bacteria, and other microscopic living organisms that kill targeted pests (such as mosquitoes) but are harmless to humans and other animals. Unlike chemical pesticides, which tend to be toxic to some degree to most living things, microbial insecticides act on a very specific target. Just as diseases that can kill a dog or cat are harmless to humans, the organisms used to kill mosquitoes affect only living creatures that are very closely related. In fact, one disadvantage of this method is that each organism will kill only one particular type of insect (it might even kill one type of mosquito and not another).

Another problem is that because the insecticide contains living organisms, it must be stored and applied properly so that the organisms do not die before they can become effective. However, in some cases, microbial insecticides offer a very safe alternative to toxic chemicals. "The era of insecticides is coming to an end," says Donald Barnard, chief of the Mosquito and Fly Research Unit at the Medical and Veterinary Entomology Research Laboratory in Gainesville, Florida. "They're still our first line of defense. But the bugs adapt very quickly to whatever we throw at them. The emphasis now is on outsmarting them."[15]

Most scientists agree that it easier to control mosquitoes before they become flying adults. In the larval stage, mosquitoes are grouped within a small area, in a habitat that can be mapped and targeted, usually away from human populations. Microbial insecticides are effective at this stage, and they avoid the need for strong chemicals.

One of the earliest and simplest methods of controlling mosquitoes is still an effective one: mosquito netting. Since most mosquitoes look for their blood meals after dark, protecting a person's sleeping area with netting can keep mosquitoes out. Sometimes netting is soaked in an insecticide solution to make it even more effective. This is a good tool for people living or staying in areas with known mosquito-borne disease problems and large mosquito populations.

Lures, Traps, and Natural Predators

Doesn't it always seem as if the moment you go outside, the mosquitoes start seeking you out? It turns out, they really do. Mosquitoes find their human and animal targets by sensing the carbon dioxide in their breath. They can detect it from up to one hundred feet away.[16] They can also find you by following the warmth of your body, using heat sensors in their antennae. (If your friends get bitten more often than you do, it is probably because their body temperatures are slightly higher.) A new type of trap that uses a combination of carbon dioxide and heat can lure mosquitoes and then kill them with an electronic pulse.

Another device, popular in the summer at restaurants, is the bug zapper. These electric lures kill mosquitoes (and other flying insects) by attracting and then electrocuting them. Although these devices may kill the few mosquitoes that get indoors, experts say they do not work well outdoors. According to the American Mosquito Control Association, bug zappers do not effectively reduce outdoor populations of mosquitoes or reduce their biting activity.[17]

Another way to control mosquitoes is by increasing the numbers of natural predators (animals that eat other animals) that like mosquitoes. Low areas where mosquitoes breed often dry up in the winter or may go for long periods without flooding. Mosquito-eating fish will disappear when this happens. When the land floods again, the mosquito population increases quickly, but then there are no fish to eat the larvae. Therefore, for years, health officials have added minnows (small fish) to replace the fish that were lost in these areas. In the summer of 1999, officials from Pasco County, Florida, and a scientist from Florida A & M University planned to update the method of increasing the fish populations by dropping minnows by helicopter into local ponds.[18]

Officials in the Bang Plad district in Thailand got kids to help solve their mosquito problem: when a new levee, or retaining wall, was built to prevent floods, it created twelve canals filled with stagnant water in the district. These canals were perfect homes for mosquitoes. Fearing an epidemic of dengue fever, the district chief, Jamnongrit Yaemkleeb, started a program to prevent a mosquito population explosion. Jamnongrit recruited kids at the Wat Samakkee Sutthawat school to scoop mosquito larvae from the canals and put them

In Thailand, canals with stagnant water were ideal homes for mosquitoes. To prevent a possible epidemic of dengue fever, a clean-up program had to be organized.

in plastic bags. Then they sold the mosquito larvae as fish food. The kids, mainly sixth graders, earned money and helped their community.[19]

Elimination of Breeding Grounds

One of the most effective ways to control mosquitoes is simply to eliminate areas where they can breed. Since mosquitoes must lay their eggs in water, emptying bodies of standing water from containers such as birdbaths, old tires, and cans is a quick and easy way to restrict their breeding. Unfortunately, it is not easy to be thorough. Even a tablespoon of water in an old soda can is enough to provide a home for two hundred mosquito larvae.[20]

In many areas of the country, dumps contain mountains of old tires, which collect water and form perfect breeding grounds for mosquitoes. A program to clean up major tire piles in North Carolina eliminated over 2 million tires by 1997.[21] Reducing the size and number of landscapes that harbor adult mosquitoes, such as those with tall weeds and overgrown vegetation, can also help. Controlling breeding in swamps, ponds, ditches, and streams takes a larger effort. Adding a thin film of oil on the surface of a body of water can prevent mosquitoes from being able to breed. The layer is so thin that it does not harm vegetation or fish.

Eliminating breeding grounds is even more complicated in other parts of the world. Robert Gwadz, head of the Laboratory of Parasitic Diseases at the National Institute of Allergy and Infectious Diseases, says that reducing the mosquito populations has worked poorly in Africa. "The mosquito isn't in clearly definable breeding sites," Gwadz says. "When you think of a mosquito, you think of swamps full of mosquitoes. And you go out and spread oil on the swamp or drain the swamp, or put fish in the swamp to eat the mosquitoes, and so you don't have a problem, right? Well, in Africa, *Anopheles gambiae*, which is the vector, may be growing in a puddle left behind when a cow stepped in the mud. . . . Or when a truck comes up the road during the rainy season and leaves a rut, the rut collects water, and mosquitoes breed in the rut. But that rut is here today and it's not going to be here two weeks from now."[22] Yet hundreds, even thousands, of mosquitoes can be produced within that period. It would be impossible to find and treat all of these tiny, temporary breeding grounds. Even if it were possible, it would not be long before there would be thousands of new areas where mosquitoes could breed.

Suppose people were able to get rid of mosquitoes completely. That would stop most mosquito-borne diseases. But would it do any harm? Scientists are always concerned about eliminating an entire species from the planet. Once it is gone, an extinct species can never be brought back. Although it appears that mosquitoes have no beneficial services to offer, they do serve as a food source for many animals, including bats. It is difficult to tell whether the environment would ultimately suffer from the absence of mosquitoes. Most experts feel that it is better to try to control their populations, and protect people from the diseases they carry, than to eliminate them completely.[23]

10

Mosquito-Borne Diseases and the Future

Why have mosquito-borne diseases become more of a threat in the United States in recent years than they used to be? Some scientists think it is because the earth is getting warmer and wetter, and mosquitoes thrive in warmth and moisture. Changes in land use due to mining, building roads, logging, irrigation projects, new dams, and human expansion into new areas put more people at risk for these diseases. Refugees fleeing wars, tourists coming home from exotic lands, and goods shipped by air can all contribute to importing more mosquitoes and the diseases they carry.

Mosquitoes are fighting hard to survive. As humans destroy more and more of their existing breeding grounds (such as swamps), mosquitoes must find new places to breed—in old tires, clogged gutters, and other areas. As populations of animals (such as horses and deer) that were traditional blood sources for mosquitoes decline, humans become their targets in greater proportions. Humans are developing increasingly more powerful and effective insecticides to kill the mosquitoes, but the mosquitoes are also adapting and developing resistance to the new chemicals. These factors make the job of controlling the mosquito population that much harder.

The diseases mosquitoes carry are also adapting. The malaria parasite has developed resistance to the drugs used to treat malaria. Malaria is now a public health problem in more than ninety countries—putting 40 percent of the world's population at risk.[1]

El Niño and Global Warming

In October 1997, it began raining in parts of northeastern Kenya and southern Somalia in Africa. It did not stop until January 1998. Earlier, mosquitoes infected with Rift Valley fever had laid virus-contaminated eggs in the area. Under normal conditions, many eggs would never have hatched, since the hatching process relies on floodwaters that are unpredictable. But this rainfall, which was sixty to one hundred times heavier than normal, triggered a massive hatch. As a result, eighty-nine thousand people got Rift Valley fever, and livestock died in astonishing numbers. More than two hundred people lost their lives due to Rift Valley fever that year.[2]

The Rift Valley fever epidemic followed an El Niño year. El Niño is the name for a particular pattern of ocean currents

97

that prevail along the west coast of South America. The currents are linked with changes in air pressure, wind strength, and ocean temperature. These changes can affect the weather as far away as Australia. Studies indicate that El Niño can cause extreme weather events such as floods or droughts. When weather changes, disease outbreaks may be larger or more severe. Mosquitoes can move into areas that were formerly too cold or too dry for them. In these new areas, people have little or no immunity to the diseases the mosquito carries. This means that more people will get sick. In addition, when people with no prior experience with a disease become infected, the symptoms they get can be more severe, and they are more likely to die from the disease. Scientists are working to improve their ability to predict weather events associated with El Niño. This will allow time for public health officials to prepare for potential outbreaks.

In addition to El Niño, a relatively new phenomenon called global warming has begun to concern scientists. Studies have shown that the earth, based on average yearly temperatures, is getting warmer. As this warming trend continues, areas that were formerly too cold to host mosquitoes are heating up. What this means is that the 1999 outbreak of West Nile fever in the northeastern United States and the surprising discovery of two cases of malaria in New York may not be unusual, isolated events in the future. As United States surgeon general David Satcher observed, "Pathogens [disease-causing organisms] have no borders."[3]

In 1999, scientists at the Goddard Space Flight Center in Greenbelt, Maryland, and the Walter Reed Army Institute of Research in Washington, D.C., published a study that linked the warming of Pacific and Indian Ocean waters with outbreaks of Rift Valley fever. The researchers examined fifty years of weather and medical information. "We discovered a cycle of Rift Valley fever outbreaks that appeared to depend on rainfall," said Kenneth Linthicum of Walter Reed.[4] But the rainfall alone did not seem to trigger the outbreaks.

The researchers found that fever outbreaks were more likely when the Indian Ocean warms at the same time that there is an El Niño, which is associated with the warming of the Pacific Ocean waters. During the El Niño, east Africa gets more rain. The researchers pointed out that satellites that can measure sea-surface temperatures, along with measurements of vegetation growth in east Africa, could help pinpoint areas where Rift Valley fever outbreaks might occur. This information might provide a two- to five-month warning period (the time between the detection of a rise in sea-surface temperatures and the eventual mosquito hatch created by the increased rainfall) for public health officials, allowing them time to vaccinate livestock and eliminate specific mosquito breeding areas.

On the Alert

August 13, 1998, was a day like any other for Scott Campbell, the entomologist from the Suffolk County Department of Health Services Arthropod-Borne Disease Laboratory who was

99

quoted earlier. That year, the division had trapped 97,378 mosquitoes, and each one had to be examined under a microscope and identified.[5] Although mosquitoes all look alike to a person trying to swat them, each species has identifying marks that help scientists classify them. On that summer day, Campbell looked through the microscope and saw something he had never seen before. This mosquito had an unusual set of white leg bands, and its body was a purplish-blue color. Campbell called James Dantonio, who had studied mosquitoes in Suffolk County for twenty-four years, but Dantonio had never seen anything like it, either.

Meanwhile, two other specimens of the same mosquito showed up. Eventually, after a number of experts up and down the East Coast had failed to identify the mosquito, the specimens ended up under the microscope of E. L. Payton, a scientist who works at the Smithsonian Institute in Washington, D.C., and who has been studying mosquitoes for the federal government since 1948. It was Payton who identified the mystery mosquito as *Aedes japonicus*, a Japanese species never before seen in North America.[6] Although scientists say the species is capable of transmitting a form of encephalitis, they do not know how big a threat, if any, it might pose to Americans. What the experience did show is that vector control programs, such as the one run by Campbell, can catch changes in the movements of mosquito species. Scientists can then be alerted when a species shows up in an unusual location.

Surveillance programs can provide information so that public health officials can deal with problems in advance, allowing them time to gather resources and prepare for possible disease outbreaks. "There is always the threat," says Campbell, "of emerging diseases like West Nile. It could have been another arbovirus that's found elsewhere in the world. Mosquitoes travel. They can be caught in airplane cargo holds. Birds migrate and are blown off course by hurricanes, so there are a lot of different aspects of danger working to keep us on our toes, basically. So I think there is the possibility of other arboviruses occurring in the U.S. They have in the past, so I don't know why they wouldn't in the future."[7]

Changing the Mosquito

One other hope remains for controlling mosquito-borne diseases: if scientists are not able to beat the mosquito, they may be able to change it. Genetic engineering, a technology that allows scientists to change the genetic structure of organisms, may turn out to be the best solution of all. For example, it may be possible for scientists to create a strain of mosquito that does not lay eggs, thus reducing future populations. Or, they might be able to develop a type that does not need blood to nourish its eggs. This new strain of mosquito would be released, to breed with existing mosquitoes, passing on its genetically altered ability.

Other scientists are experimenting with ways to place a gene in the mosquito that would make it resistant to malaria parasites. This resistance would stop the life cycle of the

101

parasite before it could spread the disease. However, Dr. Robert Gwadz, head of the Laboratory of Parasitic Diseases at the National Institute of Allergy and Infectious Diseases, admits, "It's not the kind of thing that's making great strides. One approach is to find genetic mechanisms that might interfere with development of the parasite or the virus within the mosquito."[8]

Future Research

In 1999, the World Health Organization launched a program to encourage drug companies and scientific institutions to invest additional money in finding an effective antimalarial drug for the twenty-first century. The Medicines for Malaria Venture is a public and private partnership that includes the International Federation of Pharmaceutical Manufacturers Associations, the World Bank, the Rockefeller Foundation, the Wellcome Trust, the Global Forum for Health Research, the government of the Netherlands, the Swiss Agency for Development and Cooperation, and the United Kingdom Department for International Development, in addition to WHO itself.

Researchers are using recent medical advances to develop and screen new, more effective antimalarial drugs. New technologies allow scientists rapidly to create hundreds, even thousands, of chemical combinations that can then be studied. Scientists are also examining medicinal plants for clues to developing new treatments. They are also using their improved understanding of the malaria parasite to develop ways to reduce the parasite's ability to grow, reproduce, and affect its human host.

Some researchers are looking at the malaria parasite to understand how it is evolving, or changing over time. For example, a team of researchers at the University of Edinburgh in Scotland has found that the parasite has developed a way to "chew more host."[9] Margaret Mackinnon, a researcher on the team led by Professor Andrew Read, says their experiments show that parasites that reproduce faster in the bloodstream of the host animal produce greater quantities of themselves. This increases the chances that the parasites will be picked up by a feeding mosquito and passed on to another host animal.

"We are now looking into whether the parasite will be able to find a balance," says Mackinnon. "If the parasite does too good a job of making large quantities of itself in a host animal, the host will die—and then the parasite dies as well."[10] Researchers are concerned because evolutionary changes in the parasites may produce forms of malaria that cause more severe symptoms in human hosts and create faster-moving epidemics. It may be that as humans do more to control mosquitoes and reduce the chances for them to pass on malaria parasites, the parasites will evolve into more dangerous forms in order to survive.

Robert Gwadz explains, "We really have to maintain a whole series of thrusts. Use of antimalarial drugs will be important for a long time. Under certain conditions and in concert with other things, insecticide-impregnated bed nets have great value." But Gwadz stresses, the great hope for eliminating malaria is the vaccine. "The theory is when you immunize the children against hepatitis, measles, and other childhood diseases, you would include malaria, and it would have an enormous impact." When asked how likely it is that a vaccine for malaria will be discovered, he says: "In the next few years? Not likely. In the next decade? Possible. In the next twenty years? Very possible."[11]

In 2000, President Bill Clinton announced a new program to encourage the use of existing vaccines and promote the development of new ones. The president proposed an increase in the 2001 budget for the National Institutes of Health that included increased research on vaccines for malaria. He also encouraged drug companies to develop new vaccines and to help developing countries afford to buy them.[12]

Mosquito-borne diseases will continue to present challenges, not just in developing countries, but also in America, Europe, and other parts of the world. By combining modern mosquito control techniques, surveillance, public education, and the development of improved vaccines and treatments, scientists and public health officials hope to greatly reduce the impact of this tiny but powerful pest.

Q&A

Q. How can I avoid being bitten by mosquitoes?

A. Start by wearing white clothing. Mosquitoes are attracted by both colorful clothing and body heat (increased by wearing darker colors). Use repellents, particularly those with diethyl toluamide (DEET). This chemical blocks the mosquito's ability to sense your presence. Avoid going outside after the sun begins to set, when most mosquitoes are active. Indoors, keep windows well screened and doors closed or screened. In areas that are known for large mosquito populations, keep fine netting around the bed.

Q. What can I do to help reduce the number of mosquitoes in my area?

A. Get rid of any standing water, so mosquitoes cannot breed. Change the water in birdbaths and pet dishes frequently. Empty plant dishes, baby wading pools, watering cans, tire swings, or other objects that can hold water. Pick up bottles, cans, tires, and other trash that can collect water. Drain water from pool covers and drill holes in the bottoms of recycling containers that are kept outdoors. If there is a swamp, stagnant pond, or slow-moving stream nearby, ask your local health department or mosquito control agency for help.

Q. How can I tell if the mosquito that bit me is carrying a disease?

A. You can't. You are better off trying to prevent bites, particularly if you live in an area where mosquito-borne diseases are a problem.

Q. Do other biting insects carry malaria?

A. No. They can carry other diseases, however. Ticks can carry Rocky Mountain spotted fever and Lyme disease, among others. And fleas were the carriers for the infamous Black Death, a plague that wiped out up to three quarters of the population of Europe in the fourteenth century.

Q. Are the insecticides used to control mosquitoes safe?

A. Environmental activists and public health officials argue over the relative safety of the chemicals used for killing mosquitoes. For example, malathion, the widely-used pesticide, is considered safe by public health officials who sprayed it over wide areas of New York during the West Nile virus outbreak. Yet some studies have shown that it can damage cells, perhaps causing cancer. While some of these preparations are less toxic than others, scientists say that it is important to use a variety of products to avoid having the mosquitoes become resistant to any single one. In addition, officials say they must weigh the possible risks of insecticides against the need to protect human and animal lives.

Timeline

c. 5000 B.C.—Early humans begin to settle in communities and clear land for agriculture, forcing out animals like birds, deer, and monkeys, that had acted as blood sources for mosquitoes carrying malaria and yellow fever. The mosquitoes begin preying on humans instead, since they often settle near sources of water, where mosquitoes commonly breed.

c. 400s B.C.—Malaria is a common ailment in ancient Greece, causing ill health, a falling birth rate, and low morale.

1500s—Malaria spreads to North and South America with the European explorers and the slave trade.

1590–1609—Several Dutch lens makers develop the idea of using two or more lenses to enlarge tiny objects. This invention, the compound microscope, eventually makes it possible to view the parasite that causes malaria and many other microscopic organisms.

1600s—The native people in South America discover that the bark of the cinchona tree helps eliminate the symptoms of malaria. The substance in the bark, quinine, will become a valuable weapon against malaria.

1874—Viennese pharmacist Othmar Ziedler invents the chemical compound that will become the world's most powerful weapon for killing mosquitoes: it is dichlorodiphenyl trichloro-ethylene, or DDT.

1877—Patrick Manson, a Scottish physician, discovers that mosquitoes can spread disease. He demonstrates that mosquitoes take in the tiny worms that cause elephantiasis when feeding on an infected patient and later inject the worms into healthy patients.

1880—Alphonse Laveran, a French Army surgeon, discovers the parasite *Plasmodium falciparum* in the blood of malaria patients.

1881—Carlos Finlay, a Cuban doctor, suggests yellow fever is spread by mosquito bites, but he is unable to provide proof.

1897—Ronald Ross, an India-born British doctor, finds the malaria parasite in the stomach of an *Anopheles* mosquito that had taken a blood meal from a malaria patient.

1930—South African microbiologist Max Theiler develops a vaccine for yellow fever.

1940—Paul Muller, a Swiss citizen working for a chemical company, registers Swiss patent #226,180 for the first chlorinated hydrocarbon insecticide (DDT), making possible the first large-scale attack on mosquito populations.

1950s—Chloraquine (the first antimalarial drug produced in the laboratory) becomes, after aspirin, the most commonly taken drug in the world. It saves millions of lives.

late 1950s—Resistance to chloraquine first appears. The best antimalarial drug ever available now becomes nearly useless in some areas, as the malaria parasite becomes resistant to it.

1999—An outbreak of West Nile virus in New York City shows that no area is safe from mosquito-borne diseases.

1999—Scientists at the National Institute of Allergy and Infectious Diseases produce the first detailed genetic map of *Plasmodium falciparum*, the deadliest of the malaria parasites. The map helps scientists locate genes important to drug resistance and disease severity.

2000—Scientists discover how the malaria parasite becomes resistant to drugs, raising hopes for the development of new treatments.

2000—President Bill Clinton proposes an increase in the 2001 budget for the National Institutes of Health that includes increased research into vaccines to fight malaria.

Glossary

Aedes—A genus of mosquitoes, including *Aedes aegypti*, which can carry yellow fever, dengue, and dengue hemorrhagic fever.

Anopheles—A genus of mosquitoes that can transmit malaria.

arbovirus—A type of virus that is transmitted by some kinds of insects.

arthropods—The phylum, or scientific classification, of invertebrate animals (those without backbones) that includes insects.

autopsy—A dissection and analysis of tissues of a dead animal, usually to determine the cause of death.

carrier—An animal that transports and may transmit an infectious disease but which usually does not experience any of the symptoms of the disease.

Culex—A genus of mosquitoes that includes *Culex pipiens*, which can transmit West Nile virus.

developing countries—Nations that are struggling to improve their low level of industrial production, poor economic resources, and low standard of living.

dichlorodiphenyl trichloroethane (DDT)—A pesticide that proved extremely valuable from the 1940s through the 1960s in reducing mosquito populations but which is now banned in the United States and many other countries due to environmental concerns.

Diptera—The biological order of the "true flies," which includes mosquitoes.

encephalitis—The inflammation of the brain, which can be caused by bacterial infection or any of a variety of different viruses.

entomologist—A scientist who studies insects.

entomology—The study of insects.

genetic engineering—Changing the biological makeup or behavior of a living organism by altering its genes or changing its genetic processes.

genus—The biological classification for a group of organisms that have common characteristics.

global warming—The theory that average temperatures on earth are rising, thus permanently changing the climates of many areas.

heartworm—A parasite that is transmitted by infected mosquitoes to dogs and, less commonly, to cats. The heartworm larvae go through the animal's skin, into the bloodstream to the heart.

host—A living animal or plant that provides a home for a parasite, or other disease-causing organisms.

incidence—The rate at which certain events (such as disease outbreaks) are occurring.

larva—A stage in some organisms' life cycles, occurring after the egg hatches and before the organism develops into its mature form.

merozoites—Tiny infectious organisms that are sent out by malaria parasites to invade the red blood cells of the host animal.

microfilariae—Tiny organisms produced by heartworms that circulate in the blood of an infected animal.

molt—To shed skin.

parasite—An organism that lives in or on another organism, depending upon it for food or other support.

Plasmodium—A genus of blood parasites. This group includes the four parasites that can cause malaria.

prognosis—The forecasted prospect of recovery from a disease or illness.

protozoans—A family of tiny organisms that contains some parasites, including the malaria parasites.

pupa—A stage of development in which the insect develops from a larva into an adult.

quinine—A substance that comes from the bark of the cinchona tree. It has been found to be effective in treating malaria, but it is expensive and has many side effects.

reservoir—An animal that provides a supply of disease-causing organisms but which might not show symptoms of the disease.

resistance—The ability to withstand the effects of chemicals such as drugs or insecticides designed to kill or disable, or to withstand contracting a disease.

sickle cell trait—A trait inherited by some people of African descent. It offers protection against malaria, although it causes other problems. When the gene for sickle cell is inherited from both parents, it causes sickle cell anemia.

surveillance—Keeping watch over or monitoring.

trumpets—Two tubes through which a mosquito breathes during the pupa stage.

vaccine—A preparation designed to prevent illness by producing or artificially increasing the body's immune response to a particular disease-causing organism.

vector—An animal, such as a tick, fly, or mosquito, that transmits a disease-causing organism. A virus can be a vector, too.

zoonoses—Diseases that can be passed from animals to humans and vice-versa.

For More Information

American Mosquito Control Association
Rutgers University
176 Jones Avenue
New Brunswick, NJ 08901-9998
732-932-0667
http://www.mosquito.org

Centers for Disease Control
1600 Clifton Road
Atlanta, GA 30333
800-311-3435
http://www.cdc.gov

Malaria Foundation International
46 Hillside Drive
Greenwich, CT 06830
203-862-4037
http://www.malaria.org

National Institute of Allergy and Infectious Diseases
Office of Communications and Public Liaison
Building 31, Room 7A-50
31 Center Drive MSC 2520
Bethesda, MD 20892
301-496-5717
http://www.niaid.nih.gov

United States Department of the Interior
National Wildlife Health Center
6006 Schroeder Road
Madison, WI 53711
608-270-2400
http://www.nwhc.usgs.gov

United States Department of the Interior
U.S. Geological Survey
12201 Sunrise Valley Drive
Reston, VA 20192
703-648-4000
http://www.usgs.gov/education

United States Environmental Protection Agency
Office of Pesticide Programs
Ariel Rios Building
1200 Pennsylvania Avenue, N.W.
Washington, D.C. 20460
703-305-5805
http://www.epa.gov/pesticides

World Health Organization
Regional Office for the Americas
525 23rd Street, N.W.
Washington, DC 20037
202-974-3000
http://www.who.int

Chapter Notes

Chapter 1. West Nile in New York City

1. R. Scott Nolen, "Veterinarians Key to Discovering Outbreak of Exotic Encephalitis," American Veterinary Medical Association, November 15, 1999, <http://www.avma.org/onlnews/javma/nov99/s111599a.asp> (May 29, 2000).

2. Geoffrey Cowley and Claudia Kalb, "Anatomy of an Outbreak," *Newsweek*, October 11, 1999, pp. 76–78.

3. Ibid.

4. Ibid.

5. Zdenek Hubalek and Jiri Halouzka, "West Nile Fever—A Reemerging Mosquito-Borne Viral Disease in Europe," *Emerging Infectious Diseases*, Vol. 5, No. 5, September–October 1999, Centers for Disease Control and Prevention.

6. Telephone interview with Scott Campbell, February 29, 2000.

7. Andrew C. Revkin, "Clues to an Alien Virus: Scientists Begin to Crack the Mysteries of West Nile," *The New York Times*, August 8, 2000, p. F1.

8. Martin Enserink, "EPIDEMIOLOGY: New York's Lethal Virus Came from Middle East, DNA Suggests," *Science*, November 19, 1999, pp. 1450–1451.

9. Ibid.

10. Eric Lipton, "Traces of Deadly Virus Are Found in Hibernating Mosquitoes," *The New York Times*, March 10, 2000, p. B1.

11. Ibid.

12. Revkin, p. F2.

Chapter 2. Mosquitoes and Disease

1. Andrew Curry, "Skeeters! The Horrible Truth About Mosquitoes," *The Washington Post*, August 11, 1999, p. H01.

2. Hendrik Hertzberg, "Summer's Bloodsuckers: In the Fight Against 100 Trillion Mosquitoes, the Tactics are Changing. The New Motto: Know Your Enemy," *Time*, August 10, 1992, p. 46.

3. Elizabeth Olson, "Red Cross Says Three Diseases Kill Many More Than Disasters," *The New York Times*, June 29, 2000, p. A17.

4. "A Killer in Our Sights," Africa News Service, October 22, 1999.

5. "Six Diseases Cause 90% of Infectious Disease Deaths," WHO Report on Infectious Diseases, Chapter 2, World Health Organization, 1999, <http://www.who.org/infectious-disease-report/pages/ch2text.html> (February 12, 2000).

6. Curry, p. H01.

7. Ibid.

8. "Controlling Mosquito-Borne Diseases Remains Complex," *Pest Control*, March 1, 1996, p. 40.

9. Gary Taubes, "Tales of a Bloodsucker (Asian Tiger Mosquitoes)," Vol. 19, *Discover Magazine*, July 1, 1998, pp. 124–127.

10. Michael E. Ruane, "The Buzz Is Mosquitoes; Wet Weather Brings Pest Out of Hiding," *The Washington Post*, September 8, 1999, p. A01.

11. Tom Floore, *Mosquito Information*, The American Mosquito Control Association, n.d. <http://www.mosquito.org/mosquito.html> (January 11, 2000).

12. BBC Online, "Mosquito!" BBC, October 15, 1998 <http://www.bbc.com> (October 3, 1999).

13. Wayne J. Crans, "Why Mosquitos Cannot Transmit AIDS," Rutgers Cooperative Extension Fact Sheet #FS736, n.d. <http://www-rci.rutgers.edu/~insects/aids.htm> (January 30, 2000).

Chapter 3. Mosquito-Borne Diseases in History

1. Albert S. Lyons and R. Joseph Petrucelli, *Medicine: An Illustrated History* (New York: Abradale Press, Harry N. Abrams, Inc., 1987), p. 68.

2. Ibid., p. 239.

3. Geoff Butcher, "Million Murdering Death (How Malaria Has Impacted Mankind's Progress)," *History Today*, April 1, 1998, p. 2.

4. Gary L. Miller, "Historical Natural History: Insects and the Civil War," June 29, 1999 <http://ianrwww.unl.edu/ianr/entomol/history_bug/civilwar2/gallnippers.htm> (January 31, 2000).

5. David McCullough, *The Path Between the Seas: The Creation of the Panama Canal, 1870–1914* (New York: Simon & Schuster, 1977), p. 409.

6. Nancy Duin and Jenny Sutcliffe, *A History of Medicine: From Prehistory to the Year 2020* (New York: Barnes & Noble Books, 1992), pp. 96–97.

7. Ibid., p. 97.

8. Andrew Curry, "Skeeters! The Horrible Truth About Mosquitoes," *The Washington Post*, August 11, 1999, p. H01.

9. Gordon Harrison, *Mosquitoes, Malaria and Man: A History of the Hostilities Since 1880,* (New York: E.P. Dutton, 1978), p. 164.

10. Ibid., p. 167.

11. "The Trans-Isthmian Canal and Its History," The Interoceanic Canal Museum Foundation, 1997 <http://www.sinfo.net/pcmuseum/history.html> (June 1, 2000).

Chapter 4. Yellow Fever

1. Andrew Curry, "Skeeters! The Horrible Truth About Mosquitoes," *The Washington Post*, August 11, 1999, p. H01.

2. "Yellow Fever," World Health Organization, Fact Sheet No. 100, August 1999.

3. Tracey Ober, "Rio on Disease Alert as Yellow Fever Cases Appear," Reuters, January 17, 2000.

4. Gordon Harrison, *Mosquitoes, Malaria and Man: A History of the Hostilities Since 1880* (New York: E.P. Dutton, 1978), p. 167.

5. "Yellow Fever."

6. Ibid.

Chapter 5. Malaria

1. Marguerite Johnson, reported by Bruce Cruley/Paris, "Ten-year-old Le Ngoc Giang Walks Into the Binh Khanh Village," *Time International*, May 31, 1993, p. 44.

2. Robert S. Desowitz, *The Malaria Capers: More Tales of Parasites and People, Research and Reality* (New York: W. W. Norton & Company, 1991), p. 63.

3. Ibid.

4. Jeffrey Goldberg, "Microbes on the Move," *New York Times Magazine*, October 10, 1999, p. 21.

5. Michael Balter, "AIDS Now World's Fourth Biggest Killer," *Science*, May 14, 1999, p. 1101.

6. "A Killer in Our Sights," Africa News Service, October 22, 1999.

7. National Institute of Allergy and Infectious Diseases, "NIAID and the Malaria Vaccine Initiative/PATH Sign Agreement to Accelerate Malaria Vaccine Research," *NIAID News*, February 11, 2000.

8. Lawrence K. Altman, "Diagnosis Was Malaria, but Experts Disagreed on the Source," *The New York Times*, November 9, 1999, p. F6.

9. Robert L. Hall, "Savoring Africa in the New World," *Seeds of Change*, Herman J. Viola and Carolyn Margolis, eds. (Washington: Smithsonian Institution Press, 1991), p. 171.

10. BBC Online, "Mosquito!" BBC, October 15, 1998, <http://www.bbc.com> (October 3, 1999).

11. "NIH Scientists Create First Detailed Genetic Map of Malaria Parasite," *NIAID News*, November 11, 1999.

12. "Fed: Scientists Pin Down Malaria Resistance Protein," AAP General News (Australia), February 24, 2000; Rick Callahan, "Malaria's Drug Resistance Studied," AP Online, February 23, 2000.

13. "A Killer in Our Sights."

Chapter 6. Other Mosquito-Borne Diseases

1. *The Merck Manual of Diagnosis and Therapy*, (Rahway, N.J.: Merck Sharp & Dohme Research Laboratories, 1987), pp. 190–191.

2. "Dengue and Dengue Haemorrhagic Fever," World Health Organization, Fact Sheet No. 117, November 1998.

3. "Information on Dengue Fever and Dengue Hemorrhagic Fever," Division of Vector-Borne Infectious Diseases, National Center for Infectious Diseases, Centers for Disease Control and Prevention, June 1997 <http://www.cdc.gov/ncidod/dvbid/dengue.htm> (January 11, 2000).

4. "Dengue and Dengue Haemorrhagic Fever."

5. Ibid.

6. "Information on Dengue Fever and Dengue Hemorrhagic Fever."

7. "U.S. Reports an Increase in Dengue Fever Cases," *The New York Times*, March 31, 2000, p. A23.

8. "Dengue and Dengue Haemorrhagic Fever."

9. "Rift Valley Fever," World Health Organization, Fact Sheet No. 207, December 1998.

10. "Rift Valley Fever," CDC Fact Sheet, Centers for Disease Control and Prevention <http://www.cdc.gov/od/oc/media/fact/riftvall.htm> (April 10, 1998).

11. Michael E. Ruane, "The Buzz Is Mosquitoes; Wet Weather Brings Pest Out of Hiding," *The Washington Post*, September 8, 1999, p. A01.

12. "Controlling Mosquito-Borne Diseases Remains Complex," *Pest Control*, March 1, 1996, p. 40.

13. Ibid.

Chapter 7. Animals and Mosquito-Borne Diseases

1. Dumisane Lubisi, "Rift Valley Fever Breaks Out in Mpumalanga," Africa News Service, February 9, 1999.

2. Scott Nolen, "OIE Governing Body Convenes in Paris," *Journal of the American Veterinary Medical Association*, July 15, 1999.

3. R. Scott Nolen, "Veterinarians Key to Discovering Outbreak of Exotic Encephalitis," *Journal of the American Veterinary Medical Association*, November 15, 1999, <http://www.avma.org/onlnews/javma/nov99/s111599a.asp> (May 29, 2000).

4. "Hong Kong Suspends Import of N. American Horses," Reuters, October 20, 1999.

5. Martin Enserink, "EPIDEMIOLOGY: New York's Lethal Virus Came from Middle East, DNA Suggests," *Science*, November 19, 1999, pp. 1450–1451.

6. Ridgely Ochs, "The Chicken Chase," *Newsday*, July 4, 2000, p. C3.

7. Gary Taubes, "Tales of a Bloodsucker," *Discover Magazine*, July 1, 1998, p. 124.

8. Chris Rizk, "Cats Put on Heartworm Watch," Gannett News Service, June 4, 1997, p. arc.

9. Ibid.

Chapter 8. Mosquito-Borne Diseases and Society

1. Richard Preston, "What New Things Are Going to Kill Me? As We Make Headway Against the Old Diseases," *Time*, Special Issue, Visions 21/Health & Environment, November 8, 1999, p. 86.

2. Ibid.

3. "Malaria," World Health Organization, Fact Sheet No. 94, October, 1998.

4. "Infectious Diseases Are Among the Biggest Disablers," WHO Report on Infectious Diseases, Chapter 3, World Health Organization, 1999.

5. Telephone interview with Robert Gwadz, March 14, 2000.

6. "Let's Not Save a Virulent Virus," *The Arizona Republic*, January 1, 2000, p. 4.

Chapter 9. Prevention

1. "A Killer in Our Sights," Africa News Service, October 22, 1999.

2. Ibid.

3. Ibid.

4. Robert S. Desowitz, *The Malaria Capers: More Tales of Parasites and People, Research and Reality* (New York: W. W. Norton & Company, 1991), pp. 62–64.

5. Gordon Harrison, *Mosquitoes, Malaria and Man: A History of the Hostilities Since 1880* (New York: E. P. Dutton, 1978), p. 247.

6. BBC Online, "Mosquito!" BBC, October 15, 1998 <http://www.bbc.com> (October 3, 1999).

7. Kenneth Smith, "Save Malaria Now," *The Washington Times*, September 2, 1999, p. A17.

8. "Environment/Health: The Case for DDT," Inter Press Service English News Wire, February 28, 2000.

9. Ken Silverstein, "Easy Being Green," *Mother Jones*, Vol. 24, March 1, 1999.

10. Sheryl Gay Stolberg, "Some Argue to Keep DDT to Fight Malaria," *Minneapolis Star Tribune,* September 5, 1999, p. 7A.

11. Personal minutes of public hearing, Huntington Town Hall, Huntington, New York, March 2, 2000.

12. "News from State Senator Carl L. Marcellino, Fifth Senate District," March 2, 2000.

13. Eric Staats, "Local Mosquito Control Research Draws National Attention," *Naples* [Florida] *Daily News,* July 5, 1999.

14. Ibid.

15. Hendrik Hertzberg, "Summer's Bloodsuckers: In the Fight Against 100 Trillion Mosqitoes, the Tactics are Changing. The New Motto: Know Your Enemy," *Time*, August 10, 1992, p. 46.

16. Tara Weaver-Missick, "US ARS: New Mosquito Trap in Time for Summer," M2 Press WIRE, July 14, 1999.

17. Tom Floore, "Mosquito Information," The American Mosquito Control Association <http://www.mosquito.org mosquito.html> (January 11, 2000).

18. Richard Danielson, "With the Daily Rains, Revived Mosquitoes are on the Prowl," *St. Petersburg* [Florida] *Times,* June 23, 1999, p. 1B.

19. Sukanya Saelim, "CITY LIFE: Students Sell Mosquito Larvae to Curb Rise," *The Nation* (Thailand), February 2, 2000.

20. Hertzberg.

21. "Controlling Mosquito-Borne Diseases Remains Complex," *Pest Control,* March 1, 1996, p. 40.

22. Telephone interview with Robert Gwadz, March 14, 2000.

23. Andrew Curry, "Skeeters! The Horrible Truth About Mosquitoes," *The Washington Post*, August 11, 1999, p. H1.

Chapter 10. Mosquito-Borne Diseases and the Future

1. "Malaria," World Health Organization, Fact Sheet No. 94, October 1998.

2. "El Niño and Its Health Impacts," World Health Organization, Fact Sheet No. 192, November 1998.

3. Jeffrey Goldberg, "Microbes on the Move," *New York Times Magazine*, October 10, 1999, p. 22.

4. "Study: Weather Linked to Disease," AP Online, July 15, 1999.

5. Joe Haberstroh, "A New Nuisance/LI Find, First in North America, of a Worrisome Mosquito," *Newsday*, February 14, 1999, p. A03.

6. Ibid.

7. Telephone interview with Scott Campbell, February 29, 2000.

8. Telephone interview with Robert Gwadz, March 14, 2000.

9. Personal communications with Margaret MacKinnon via e-mail, February 16, 2000.

10. Ibid.

11. Telephone interview with Robert Gwadz, March 14, 2000.

12. "Clinton Unveils New Vaccine Initiative," White House Fact Sheet, *U.S. Newswire*, January 28, 2000.

Further Reading

Bailey, Jill. *Mosquito*. Jordan Hill, U.K.: Heineman Library, 1998.

Desalle, Rob, ed. *Epidemic!: The World of Infectious Diseases*. New York: The New Press, 1999.

Gaines, Ann Graham. *The Panama Canal*. Berkeley Heights, N.J.: Enslow Publishers, Inc., 1999.

McDonald, Mary Ann. *Mosquitoes*. Chanhassen, Minn.: Childs World, 2000.

Yount, Lisa. *Epidemics*. San Diego, Calif.: Lucent, 1999.

Internet Addresses

Malaria Information
Division of Laboratory Medicine at Royal Perth Hospital (Australia)
<http://www.rph.wa.gov.au>

New Jersey Mosquito Homepage
<http://www-rci.rutgers.edu/~insects/njmos.htm>

Viral Encephalitis
The Mayo Clinic
<http://www.mayohealth.org/home?id=HQ01600>

West Nile Virus
Centers for Disease Control and Prevention
<http://www.cdc.gov/ncidod/dvbid/westnile/index.htm>

West Nile Virus Resources for the General Public
Cornell University
<http://www.cfe.cornell.edu/risk/WNVmainpage.html>

Index

M

Mackinnon, Margaret, 103
malaria, 7, 8, 19, 20, 24, 32–38,
    41, 42, 48, 49–59, 66, 76, 77,
    81–82, 83, 97, 101–104
Malaria Project, 86
Malaria Vaccine Initiative, 82
malathion, 86
Manson, Patrick, 33–34, 36, 65
Marcellino, Carl, 86–88
McNamara, Tracey, 11–14
Medicines for Malaria Venture, 102
mosquito. *See also* species.
    anatomy, 20–21, 27–28
    bite, 7, 8, 9, 20–21, 22, 27, 28,
        29, 30, 31, 35, 38, 39–41,
        64, 92
    breeding grounds, 9, 23, 24,
        32–33, 41, 54, 78–79, 89,
        92–95, 96–97, 99
    control, 15, 17, 82–95, 100,
        103, 104
    life cycle, 16–17, 24–27
    netting, 9, 40, 91
    predators of, 92–94
    repellents, 9, 88–90
    spraying, 12, 86–88, 89–90
    surveillance, 14, 15, 101, 104
    traps, 14, 92
mosquito-borne diseases
    animals and, 7, 9, 11–12, 13,
        14, 15, 16, 18, 21, 22, 27,
        28, 36, 38, 44, 45, 54, 63,
        66–73, 76, 82, 85, 87–88,
        89–90, 96–97, 99
    diagnosis, 46–47, 55, 63, 64,
        70–71, 73
    environmental impact, 67, 74,
        78–79, 84–88, 89–91, 95,
        96–97, 98
    economic impact, 18, 43, 68,
        74, 76–78, 85–86
    future research, 102–104

geographic ranges, 7, 14, 16,
    45, 46, 52, 53–54, 60, 61,
    63, 65, 75–76, 83
historical impact, 19, 20,
    32–33, 38, 43, 44
outbreaks, 7, 15, 16, 17, 24, 38,
    45, 63, 65, 67, 68–69, 70,
    74, 76, 78, 86, 98, 99, 101.
    See also epidemics.
prevention, 9, 12, 14, 15, 19,
    41–42, 52, 78–79, 80–95
social impact, 18, 74–79,
    85–86, 87, 88, 96
spread, 16–17, 34, 39–40, 44,
    65, 68, 76, 96–97
symptoms, 8, 9, 11, 45, 46–47,
    49, 54, 55, 63, 64, 71
transmission, 8, 21, 27–31, 35,
    36, 38–40, 71–72
treatment, 8–9, 37, 47, 55–58,
    63, 64, 70, 72–73, 104
types, 7, 61, 65
Muller, Paul, 83

N

National Academy of Sciences, 84
National Center for Infectious
    Diseases, 17
National Institute of Allergy and
    Infectious Diseases, 17, 57, 79,
    94, 102
National Institutes of Health, 104
Naval Medical Research Center, 81
Ninivaggi, Dominic, 87–88

P

Panama Canal, 41–42, 43
parasites, 27, 34, 35, 36, 38,
    50–51, 52, 54, 55, 56, 57–59,
    66, 81, 82, 97, 101–103
Payton, E.L., 100
pesticides, 12, 14, 74, 86, 90. *See
    also* insecticides.
Phlebovirus, 63